To Be Inspired

Stories of Courage and Hope after Brain Injury

By David & Sarah Grant

To Be Inspired ©2016 by David & Sarah Grant

Produced in the United States of America. No part of this book may be used or reproduced in any manner without written permission by the author whatsoever except in the case of reprints in the context of reviews.

On the Web: www.TBIHopeandInspiration.com

Book Production Services by David Grant Books. For more information about book production services, please visit www.davidgrantbooks.com

All Rights Reserved.

Contents

Introduction 9

Look Where You Want to Go, Rosemary *Rawlins* 10

Extra Birthdays, *Donna Hafner* 14

After the Crash, Carole *Starr* 18

Looking for a Sign, *Wendy Proctor* 22

Against All Odds, Laura *Chagnon* 26

Blessings Abound, *Jennifer White.* 32

Walking in the Dark, *Michael Strand* 36

Meet the Nowinator, *Mike Jennings* 40

Lights, Camera, Action, *Cheryl Green* 42

Avoiding the New Neighbor, John *Byler* 46

What I Wish I had Known, *Amy Zellmer* 50

Ten Things Brain Injured Patients Want their Doctor to Know, *Nancy Hueber* 54

Four Pins and a Plate, *Doug Rowe* 58

Living a Purpose-Filled Life, Joan *Miller* 66

A Glimpse into my TBI, *Dr. Katherine Kimes* 70

Seven Schools – One Degree, *Melissa Robison* 76

Living in a War Zone, *Nancy Bauser* 80

Creating Success in our Lives, *Jeff Sebell* 84

I Am a Miracle, *Natalie Griffith* 88

My Experience with Brain Injury, *Grant Evans* 92

Double Trauma, *Norma Myers* 100

The Brain Injury I Never Knew I Had, *Sara Lewis* 104

Rethinking the Holidays, *Deborah Schlag* 110

From Tragedy to Triumph, *Jessica E. Taylor*................................116

Miracles Happen, *Valerie Van Selous* 120

Learning to Like the New Me, *Shannon Sharman* 128

A New Perspective, *Donna Becke* 134

No was Never an Option, *Brian Maram* 136

Shattering the One Year Myth, *David A. Grant* 140

Learning to Become Useful Again, *Steve Brydon* 144

Living One Day at a Time, *Drew Palavage* 148

Journaling a New Story after Brain Injury, *Barbara Stahura* ...154

Healing your Heart after a Brain Injury, *Barbara J. Webster* ...158

Finding Gems in the Mud, *Nathalie Kelly* 162

Embrace the Day, *Terri Mongait* 170

My Journey to Regain Wellness, *Amiee Duffy* 174

Left for This, *Kylie Hammon* 178

Meet Our Contributors 189

Introduction

Several years ago, life forever changed for my wife Sarah and me after I sustained a traumatic brain injury (TBI). Over the years since the accident, we have learned that TBI affects the entire family.

No one asks to have their entire lives upended in two ticks of a clock, but it happens to more people than you would ever think. The CDC estimates that up to 3.4 million Americans sustain a brain injury every year. The numbers are staggering.

As our roles as brain injury advocates continued to emerge over the last few years, we found ourselves in the most unlikely position of becoming magazine publishers. Every month, TBI HOPE Magazine is distributed to a worldwide readership.

The stories included in this book have been selected from our contributing writers. They are moms, dads, sons, daughters, teachers and true inspirers.

Our hope is that you can come away from this book with a better understanding of what life is like for all affected by traumatic brain injury. Our goal is a simple one as we want others to see that a meaningful life is indeed possible after a TBI.

~ David & Sarah Grant

Look Where You Want to Go

I wasn't always so fearful. There was a time when I felt secure in the world, when I thought I had control over my own destiny. That time ended on April 13, 2002.

Before then, I didn't know that one moment could change the course of many lives, that a hard knock on the head could erase precious memories or alter a person's personality, that our brain alone programs who we are by speeding up or slowing down our mental power, determining our behavior, and how well our body functions in the world.

I used to think the heart was in charge. I was a romantic. It was the brain all along. The brain alone can stop the heart.

Since the day my husband's head smacked the hard pavement after a fast car hit him, I've worked long and hard to let go of fear. Just yesterday, as Hugh drove me along Interstate 64 in a downpour, my right foot pressed into the floor hard enough to cramp my thigh when another car cut us off. I stopped breathing when the brakes hesitated for a moment as my husband hit the brakes. As I lurched forward, I saw myself fly through the windshield like I have a thousand times since the day he was hit. It's not only the crash that haunts me. My deepest fear lies in knowing the months and years of devastation that can follow one horrific split second.

Because of my book and work on BrainLine.org, many caregivers contact me personally about their unrelenting fear of the future. Many say they keep reliving the day their loved one almost died. They are relieved when I suggest they may have secondary stress—something concrete with a name. A caregiver's personality can change pretty drastically and understandably after he or she witnesses a loved one's brush with death. Secondary stress might look like insomnia and hypervigilance or the inability to separate from a loved one's pain. A caregiver might morph from a relatively carefree person into an anxiety-ridden, overprotective, and controlling person.

We read articles all the time with headlines like: "Ten Tips for a Better Life" or "How to Stop Stressing for Good." But the truth is, getting over the life-changing injury of a loved one is impossible—we don't get over it, but we can learn to live with it and find peace and meaning for ourselves. This healing requires a commitment to our own neglected health, visits to the doctor, following orders, and counseling. We need to take the medicine we are so used to giving! I know because it took me fifteen months to figure this out, and even then, I wasn't really taking care of myself—I was putting out fires. I would say, "It's time I slow down and make time for myself," but I didn't always do it. I made excuses.

I didn't realize that I had to stop seeing the accident everywhere I looked before I could see the life that was going on around me. My husband, Hugh, once coached a mountain biker, "Look where you want to go. If you look at the tree, you'll hit the tree." I kept looking at the accident as if I could find a way to rewind it, to undo it, to figure it out. It loomed like an obstacle I could not get around.

When I got sick and tired of being me, of feeling angry, bitter, sad, sleepless, and worried all the time, I searched day and night for a space between the trees where the sunlight found a path, and one day it was there. I walked away from one life and created another. When you feel desperate, please keep looking until you can see beyond the wreckage of that one moment in time. Because when you do, you'll create an opening in your life where you can begin to live and like yourself again.

Extra Birthdays

Another year has passed and with it another birthday. I turned fifty-four. It was the fourth birthday that I was not expected to see. I don't know why, but it hit me hard this year. It's a pretty safe bet that if you are reading this now, you probably have an extra birthday or two under your belt. Perhaps a couple of extra Christmases as well. Maybe you love someone with a brain injury and you have been able to experience the joy of sharing an additional birthday or special event that no one had expected them to live to see.

In November of 2011, I was just fifty years old when I had an unexpected and massive heart attack.

My heart attack was immediately followed by multiple strokes that left me in a coma for two weeks at the University of Washington Hospital in Seattle. ICU and hospital experiences are shared by many survivors and their families. My family was not immune to spending nearly two months in them before I was eventually released.

They said I tried my best to die and had to be resuscitated thirty-one different times. My poor ticker was determined to give up the ghost, but the medical team kept finding ways to bring me back to life. In the course of those episodes, I suffered many strokes throughout various areas of my brain. My prognosis was very poor. The medical staff said that if I were to survive, my cognitive abilities were expected to be minimal at best. The doctor said I might be able to gossip or possibly even watch a baseball game on TV. Rest assured, this is not exactly the type of life that I was leading prior to my injuries.

Thankfully, my family chose to roll the dice and decided that heroic measures would continue. And so they did.

Heroic measures continued until my family was told that there was no hope left. I wasn't going to come out of the coma. The images of my brain looked ominous with all of the white blobs showing up quite distinctively against the dark MRI scans. My family was told it was finally time to let me go. It was time for me to pass.

I can't begin to imagine that conversation, and cringe to think of their pain in that final moment of decision. "Should we or shouldn't we?" Eventually, they came to a consensus and a conclusion. It was time to pull the plug. Excruciating goodbyes were said at my bedside, with tears streaming. All the while, I lay motionless, just as I had since the moment that my heart attack hit.

It was fortunate that I was an organ donor and had signed the donor card over three decades earlier. My family had agreed to allow them to harvest my organs, per my wishes. This turned out to be a lucky stroke of luck for me.

The Organ Harvesting Team was running a bit late, so I was still on full life-support when my heart unexpectedly started racing. This required three more good shocks to get it stabilized again in order for my organs to be viable. YAY for me. Those three good shocks apparently jump-started my brain too. Somewhere in the next ninety minutes, I fought my way back from the near dead.

My family had returned to my bedside. I suddenly moved a toe, ever so slightly. You can imagine their disbelief. I had been motionless for all of this time, literally on the chopping block. Suddenly and against all odds, I was showing signs of life. The Do Not Resuscitate notice was immediately pulled off of the wall above my head. My doctors rushed in to see the miracle in progress. My intubation was pulled out within the hour. Miracles are another thing that many of us survivors and families have in common as well.

Each additional birthday or holiday that I now experience is cherished and treasured. We all only have so many. I've learned the hard way not to take any of them for granted. I think it hit harder this year because I have the gift of distance from the trauma now. These were four years that I was not expected to have - four years of life. In the early days, I only saw what I couldn't do and who I no longer was.

But slowly, over time, I've learned that life does continue, sometimes in spite of ourselves. No, it often isn't the same. But nonetheless, it's much better than the alternative. Are birthdays more cherished than they've ever been? You tell me.

After the Crash

After brain injury, we strive to get back to "normal", to "the way life used to be". Anything less seems like failure. However, brain injury has changed us forever and the more we compare our "new selves" to our "old selves", the worse we feel. Keeping a portfolio of my progress and accomplishments has helped me to stop comparing, accept and even to embrace my "new self" after brain injury.

I've always been one to save mementos and organize them into scrapbooks. I like visual cues to remember my past and take pride in what I've done. In my former life as an educator, I kept a professional portfolio which included documentation of all my teaching-related accomplishments.

In 1999, I sustained a brain injury in a car accident. For several years, I focused mostly on relearning basic life tasks. I completely forgot that my professional portfolio existed. One day, by chance, I re-found it. Reading through my former life was devastating. Here was documentation of all the things I used to be able to do but now couldn't. I had been a professional educator and now I was reduced to being a professional patient. Reading the portfolio triggered the overwhelming grief I felt about my lost life. At the time, my portfolio proved to me all the harsh judgments I then believed about myself—that I was inadequate, a failure, a cracked version of my former self who would never again achieve anything worthwhile.

Every day, I would pull out my portfolio, think about all the losses and compare this unwelcome "new Carole" to the much better "old Carole". The more I looked at my portfolio, the worse I felt. I knew it wasn't healthy to do, but I couldn't seem to help myself.

After about a month of this, I had an epiphany, one that changed the way I thought about myself and my brain injury. My counselor and I had been working on a "thought stopping" technique, to rein in my tendency to judge myself so harshly. One part of the technique involved testing the truthfulness of my thoughts. I'd placed copies of the technique throughout my house, so I would remember to use it. One day, as I looked at my portfolio and sobbed over my lost life, I saw the thought stopping technique. I asked myself, "Is it true that I no longer have any accomplishments?"

With a sudden jolt of awareness, I realized that even though I could no longer do the activities documented in my portfolio, there were still multiple activities that the "new me" had accomplished. I had written a few poems, one of which had been published on a brain injury website. I had discovered a new, great satisfaction in using my hands to make crafts. I'd volunteered for about thirty minutes a week at an organization where I used to work.

With help from my Occupational Therapist, I had a six week menu plan, which allowed me to regain control of my cooking. While those accomplishments were quite different from my previous ones, I was indeed extremely proud of them. I realized that those successes deserved my recognition just as much as the ones from my previous life.

At that time in my recovery, compiling and categorizing those accomplishments into a put-together portfolio was beyond my organizational skills. So, I simply placed documentation of those early successes in a folder in my desk. I called it the "Stuff I'm Proud of" folder. Over time I added to it—more writing, pictures of crafts I'd made, events I'd attended, speeches I'd given—anything large or small that I was proud of and/or represented progress in my recovery. Eventually, that folder bulged with accomplishments.

A couple years later, I was asked to participate in a workshop about creativity and brain injury. I decided to put together a more formal portfolio for that workshop. I purchased a large 3-ring binder and my Recreation Therapist helped me sort and divide my Stuff I'm Proud Of folder into several categories—Writing, Crafts, Brain Injury Speaking, Volunteering and Other (for anything that didn't fit neatly into a category). Each section was organized from earliest to most recent activities. Just seeing that Stuff I'm Proud Of folder all together in an organized portfolio gave me tremendous feelings of pride, satisfaction and accomplishment. I named this portfolio After the Crash.

After the Crash is a visual reminder of all the progress I've made, the pride I feel in my accomplishments and the sense of purpose I have now as a brain injury speaker and leader of Brain Injury Voices. It's so rewarding to compare the early activities documented in the back of my portfolio to the more recent ones in the front. Many once challenging activities are now easy. During times when I feel sad, and all I can see is what I still cannot do, my portfolio shows me just how far I've come.

As I've documented my small successes gradually building into larger ones, I've learned to stop comparing the new Carole to who I was before my brain injury. My old portfolio's home is now a box in my attic. Instead of trying to get back to the way life used to be, I focus my energies into creating a new life, one that works within the limitations of my brain injury. "After the Crash" reminds me that the way forward after brain injury is to focus on what I CAN do and build from there.

 My portfolio has played a critical role in helping me to accept and like my new self after brain injury. If you've been inspired by this essay, I hope you will think about all that you've accomplished since your brain injury and begin your own Stuff I'm Proud Of folder.

Looking for a Sign

I loved my job as program director working with youth. Life was good! All that changed on July 28, 2008. While on a field trip with my students, I stepped off the school bus and was struck by a passing vehicle, sustaining broken bones, lacerations and a traumatic brain injury. It happened days before my only daughter was to be married. The wedding was cancelled, and I never got the chance to see my beautiful daughter walk down the aisle with the boy she was in love with, wearing the beautiful dress that we had spent many hours searching for.

Survivors struggle with many emotions following an injury, including sadness, hopelessness, deep loss and more. I felt all those along with a deep anger that consumed me, yet I was powerless to change how I felt.

One day, I picked up an artist's brush. I wanted to have a tangible portrait of how I felt, an expression of the anger that ate away inside me. From the canvas emerged a reflection of how I was feeling and suddenly, something indescribable happened inside me! For the first time in many months, I actually felt happy! I felt liberated! In the days that followed, whenever I looked at that sketch, it just made me feel better.

I continued sketching, sometimes penning words on the canvas. And always, when I was creating art, I felt that same sense of accomplishment and feeling of peace. On days when the anger seemed unbearable, I would pull out my art supplies and paint, but I felt my work was not that great, so I kept it hidden. One of the common themes with all my artwork, was the obvious reflection of deep anger and sadness and each portrait had tears falling from one eye.

I came across a posting for an art retreat and I made plans to attend. I was drawn to the beautiful colors in one particular artist's work, so I applied for her workshop and made arrangements to attend. I was so nervous on the day of the workshop.

This was a big step for me. As fate would have it, I was the first student that she asked to share where I was from, and why I was there. I loved the beautiful work this artist had created and I knew she was accomplished in her field. She was published and well-known for her beautiful artwork that is so full of color and life. I don't really recall what I said, but I managed to mumble something.

Through snippets of conversation during the workshop, I realized that there were many accomplished artists present, including the artist seated beside me who used art as therapy when working with clients in her rehabilitation program. These were clients who sounded a lot like me, who were facing challenges as a result of injuries!

I must explain, I am the type of person that always looks for a "sign" and this day was no different. Along with trying to hide my disability and blend in with the other artists in the workshop, I was also starting to feel inadequate. I gave myself a good talking to, as I was determined to see this day through. On the inside, my anxiety was threatening to ruin the day. "If I could just have some small sign," I said to myself… "Anything to get me through this day."

Suddenly, the artist announced that she often had a drawing and gave away "gifts" during her workshops. Sometimes, they would be special paints, maybe brushes, perhaps a selection from her painting portfolio. We were to place our name in a container and she would draw out a winner. Well, imagine my surprise when I was chosen first to receive a "gift!" When she presented me with the gift, I felt a mixture of elation and disappointment. Elation, because I connected with the artwork immediately, and disappointment because it was not the beautiful colors that drew me to this artist.

"I like it," I said, "but it is not yours." For those who don't know, what often happens with survivors of a traumatic brain injury, we think a thought, and before we know it, we've blurted it out!

The artist smiled and nodded and said, "It is my artwork." I quickly blinked away my tears, and I can tell you it is the most precious piece of artwork that I own. The painting is of a young woman and you can feel the emotion in the piece. She even has a tear streaming down her face! At that moment, I knew I was right where I was supposed to be.

Against All Odds

My name is Laura. I am a TBI survivor and quite lucky to be here today writing this. Actually, I'm not typing this with my own hands, I need the help of others to do any physical tasks.

I'm 51 years old and my life started off in good health. My major problem growing up as an adolescent was shyness. There was a lot of difficulty mixing in socially at school and I was bullied every day. During lunch in the cafeteria, I would be the only student sitting alone because I was like that puzzle piece that just didn't fit. It caused a lot of loneliness and frustration therefore, I needed to vent all of my built-up emotion.

English was my strongest subject in school. I enjoyed writing, so I began writing poetry. Never did I realize how my situation at this stage of my life would be so important later on. Ironically, those dark days would open up new doors later down the road.

I completed high school, despite the bullying, but my self-esteem was left tormented. My life needed direction in order to become a stronger person. So, I chose to enter the military, the U.S. Army to be exact. I'm a very patriotic individual, so this venture seemed to be a perfect fit. My bags were packed and my destination was Fort Jackson, South Carolina. Basic training here I come. There was one slight problem, I always suffered from insomnia.

One day, my job was to carry a line of cable through the woods. I had gone days without sleep and was simply exhausted. So, I dropped the cable in the woods and went back to my barracks and collapsed. The drill instructor found me there and doctors realized continuing on with basic training could lead to more serious health issues. I was given a medical discharge and sent back home.

I had to decide what my next path in life would be, so college seemed to be a logical choice. Soon I was enrolled in Springfield Technical Community College. I wanted to become a medical assistant. Everything was going in a positive direction, my grades were good and I was excited. At 25-years-old, I could see myself graduating soon, getting a job and an apartment. Being independent would be a dream come true. My 26th birthday was soon approaching, November 4th, 1989 turned out to be a life-changing day.

My mom bought me a gray suede jacket and a white leather pocketbook. I always did things spontaneously, and this day was no different. I took off and went to Boston on my own, driven by excitement with this adventure. In Boston, I decided to go window shopping and see the sights. Being a college student, there really wasn't very much money to spend, but I didn't care.

This fated November day started off sunny, but soon I was entangled by the dark shadows of that fall day in New England. It turned out to be the most traumatic nightmare in my life. I felt a tug on the new white purse that was strapped over my shoulder. Immediately, red flags went up and I envisioned being robbed. Since I didn't have very much money, it wouldn't really be the worst thing that could happen.

I was spun around and I stared into the eyes of two men. In a matter of moments, my life was changed forever. My memory of the incident is very scarce. They brought me to a secluded area and I don't remember what occurred since they fractured my skull. The assailants left my crumpled body on the streets of Boston to die, then left the scene never to be caught. Boston police found me and thought my gift of life was stolen.

However, someone was holding my hand and not allowing me to die. That was God. I suffered terrible injuries, but He had a path for me. It is ironic how through different stages of my life, I was trying to create my own path. God intervened and set the right one before me.

My body was broken, and now I was a legally blind quadriplegic with a traumatic brain injury. Doctors gave me little chance of regaining much of my former cognitive ability. Was I going to give up on life? No way! My ever-loving God allowed me to live and my goal was to realize he was opening a new door for me, even though it would take me more than four years to even see it. I went through physical, occupational, and speech therapy at numerous rehab centers. Finally, in 1992, I was able to return to live with my parents.

What would I do with my new life? I couldn't work a standard job with my physical skills being stripped. I needed caregivers 24/7. I guess I was in a predicament, or was I? Remembering back to those adolescent years, I enjoyed writing poetry. Guess what? Now I had the time to delve back into that with a vengeance. My process was dictating to my caregivers, and they would write down the words. When a poem was completed, it would be saved on my computer. I did this day after day, even submitting some of my works to local publications. A writer for the local newspaper even did an article on me in his human interest column and entitled it "In Poetry She Finds a New Spirit." I was excited and kept on writing with the goal of allowing others to read my words. Perhaps I could even publish a book. But that seemed to be quite a lofty goal.

Then in 2013, I met an angel. He was a short, stocky man who wore glasses; perhaps not your typical angel, his halo even a bit askew. His name is Todd Civin. My soul mate had purchased a book that Todd co-wrote. We contacted Todd with the idea that he would be able to bring a sampling of my poems to his publishing company and have them evaluated. We met for lunch and had a nice conversation. I explained to him my story and my dreams of becoming a published poet. I gave him about 20 of my poems to bring back to his publishing company. He said he would give us a call in about a week. A week went by and we didn't receive that much-awaited phone call.

My life had been full of disappointments up to that time, and this seemed no different. Then, two weeks later, I heard the phone ring. "Hello Laura, this is Todd Civin from Mascot Books. Well, your story is quite incredible and we think your poetry is absolutely amazing. The public needs to know about you and read your beautiful words. We would like to publish a book of your inspiring poetry."

At last, a long-awaited dream came true. In April of 2014, "Never Touched a Pen" the inspired poetry of Laura Chagnon was released. Twenty-five years after my accident, I found out that dreams really do come true. I am proud to say that I am a traumatic brain injury survivor and I continue to strive each day with God always close to me and always by my side.

Blessings Abound

On July 28, 2000, I went from being an executive at a marketing company who serviced a number of national nonprofit organizations, to an unemployed housewife in a period of 24 hours. The cause: an intracerebral hemorrhage on my brain stem.

Living in a downtown apartment in Atlanta, GA, I lost consciousness and subsequently called 911. After speaking with an emergency operator who tried to calm me down by telling me I wasn't dying, I was rushed to a hospital via ambulance where I did die and was resuscitated en-route to the emergency room.

The final diagnosis was severe coma in the presence of a massive interventricular hemorrhage. I had a right frontal ventriculostomy to eradicate the blood clot that sat on my brain stem, and a sub-occipital craniotomy to evacuate the hematoma, and duraplasty. I then had a ventriculoperitoneal shunt performed. I was intubated on the ride to the hospital and was admitted to the emergency room without brain stem reflexes.

My husband was told that I only had a 4% chance of survival. Following the surgeries, a feeding tube was placed. Due to right lower lobe pneumonia I was treated with multiple intravenous antibiotics. Six days later the pneumonia started to clear and I was being weaned off of the ventilator that was keeping me alive.

As the pneumonia cleared and I started tolerating procedures more so than the days before, speech, occupational, and physical therapy staff were asked to evaluate me for possible rehab. On the 18th hospital day, I was transferred from the ICU to a bed on the hospital floor. On the 25th hospital day, I was transferred to the acquired brain injury unit at a local rehab center where I was in stable condition but definitely not out of the woods. I was in rehab for several months, where I had to relearn how to walk, talk, eat, swallow, and perform simple tasks.

I also had to learn how to lean on others for help - one thing I was always too proud to do prior to the hemorrhage. Cognitively, I was a different person. I could no longer work and was placed on long term disability. I really wanted to work, however. I yearned for the day that I had to develop an annual marketing and budget plan for my clients or travel to a dozen different states pitching a new fundraising idea.

In a period of 24 hours, my future was determined for me. The days of easily navigating my life had ended with my traumatic brain injury. I now had to seriously think about every step I take since my balance has been negatively impacted. My sequencing ability was seriously compromised as I frequently asked myself what came first – socks or shoes, shampoo or conditioner. I took everything that I knew prior to the brain injury for granted and had to relearn rudimentary tasks that had taken me a lifetime to learn. I lost those things in a matter of 24 hours.

What I never thought would happen actually happened. My fear of dying reared its ugly head when I was told I had died on the way to the hospital. The choice of whether I should have children was made for me when, after my brain injury, my surgeon recommended that I not have children. After the brain injury, I began to appreciate things more. I had a new perspective on my life and learned what true love is from the kindness I was shown from my family. My husband was so loyal and extremely committed to my survival. He made me get up when I just wanted to die. He made me walk when I just wanted to give up. I try to thank him for his loyalty but he is such a humble man, he simply asks me "How could I not have helped you?" I have siblings that helped me deal too. I'll never know completely what my brain injury did to all of them. I think, however, we all grew some that day.

After the day of the brain injury and it was clear that I would live through the nightmare, I set off to recreate my life as someone who would more than likely never work again. I took classes to be a master gardener. I learned how to quilt and have made at least twenty, so far. I dedicated my mental energy into being the best wife ever and believe that it is my husband's time to shine. It is his turn, and he is doing very well. I started seeing a new outlook on life. Colors are brighter, relationships are sweeter and my success is no longer measured by how much money I make or what kind of position I hold at work. My success is measured by how kind I am to people and how much of myself I can give.

This is truly different than when I lived in downtown Atlanta in a high rise apartment and worked seven days a week. I do feel some survivor's remorse, but I am happy to be alive! The guilt I feel from putting my family through so much pain is starting to lessen a bit. It has given way to thankfulness for being alive. How many people get a "do-over" in life? It was the worst time and the best time, because I did not die but was left with a question… How am I going to live the rest of my life? I am certain that I am most likely unrecognizable to those who knew me prior to the brain injury. Not physically, since I pretty much look the same, but emotionally. Rather, I am now a softer, kinder, less aggressive and more introspective person. And of course I still deal with painful headaches, cognitive deficits, and balance issues. But, the number of good days are becoming greater than the bad ones. For this I am happy.

Walking in the Dark

Living with a brain injury is feeling what it must be like to be immortal. With no memory of a past there can be no notion of a future. Forever in the present; an eternity of now. Actually, brain injury is slightly different. I have a memory, but I have no certainty that my memory is valid. At any time I can discover that what I remember is not what anyone else remembers and when this happens it is always me who is wrong. This makes using my judgment a complete joke.

Most consistently, this is an issue when I am fatigued. There are many things I have difficulty doing well or even safely, when I am tired. But it is rarely as simple or obvious as being able or unable to do something. It is a matter of chance; a matter of odds. Do I feel well enough to drive? Do I feel sharp enough to handle a difficult transaction? How about when my significant other wants to discuss something with me? Am I too tired to respond rationally and responsibly? Am I more likely to lose my temper? It would be nice if in real life I could just say, "You know, those are really valid concerns, but I'm just too tired to talk about it right now." However, in the lively chemistry of human relationships, that is rarely a response that it occurs to me to make. It is usually much later, when I realize in hindsight, that that is in fact what I should have said.

The problem here is that there are very few absolutes. It is rarely as obvious as, "No, I can't fly like a bird, so I'm not jumping off this bridge." It is commonly something like "I really shouldn't drive when I'm this tired, so I don't think I can run this errand."

The biggest problem for me now however, is not those issues as they truly are, but as they appear. They appear convenient. Although their actual convenience may be only coincidental, it seems to other people that I am only using my brain injury to get out of something I don't want to do. Sometimes I am not even really sure if it is an actual concern or just convenience. Maybe I really would rather not go shopping for my brother's birthday present… Or maybe it really is too late for me to be out driving.

So, if even I am not sure, then I certainly can't blame other people if they wonder, ask, or accuse me of making an excuse out of my brain injury. It was 1989 when I had my accident and still every day I have to deal with lingering effects of my brain injury. I am pretty high functioning and most of the time I can keep my brain injury from being the most noticeable thing about me. But then my closest friends will tell me I can't use my brain injury as an excuse anymore (mere acquaintances would never say that). When they say that I tend to want to agree with them, but then something will occur that reminds me that saying I don't have a brain injury is denying I have a brain injury, and that can have serious repercussions when I stop using the various tactics and techniques I have cleverly devised as compensatory strategies to get through the day.

Once again, the most frustrating thing is that there is no right answer and there is no wrong answer. There are only shades of might have and should have. Regrets pile up with little hope of profiting by experience because everything is relatively risky. Everything is contingent on variables that are undefinable in the present. I live caged in the NOW with no memory. There is no anticipation but what the mind imagines. In a hostile environment, that means dread. Living with a brain injury is like walking in a dark room unable to see the furniture.

Meet the Nowinator

I recently discovered a new personality trait: I've become a Nowinator! What I mean is that I now do things right away, if I can. Let me explain.

Deciding to do something later requires you to remember to do so. You may say, I'll write it down so I have a record of it. The problem is that if you write everything down, you can find yourself overwhelmed by notes. By just going ahead and doing it now, you don't have to worry about remembering it. Also, although something may seem simple at first to remember, later you may find that you forgot to do it. I know I have!

I used to be the exact opposite. I would wait until the last minute to do things. I was a classic procrastinator. Maybe it was a game to see how late I could start something and still get it done on time. Now, after my brain injury, I need to be really efficient doing everything. Here's what I do now…

Even if something can wait and I can do it later, I'll just do it now. This way, I don't have to remember later. I think less energy is required to just do it now. An example is when I'm running low on medication and I need to have it refilled in about a week. Rather than wait until the last minute, I get it refilled right away. So I made up a new term for myself. Now, I'm a Nowinator!

Lights, Camera, Action

In 2011, I became a filmmaker without ever intending to. I have always loved movies, but I had a career as a speech-language pathologist back then. Or so I thought.

Ten days before my first speech therapy job, a serious bike crash put my career on hold. My experiences as a patient in rehab were not very positive. I didn't want to recreate them for someone else, so I left the field before starting. Also, the more people with brain injury disabilities I met, the more I enjoyed spending time with them as peers, not helping them regain skills like I was trained to do. After rehab, I spent time with some disabled artists in Portland, Oregon and accidentally became a filmmaker.

It started with a short comedy, "Cooking with Brain Injury." In it, a friend and I recreated some of my problems in the kitchen. We staged a daytime cooking show where everything goes wrong.

I thought my filmmaking career would end there. But people with brain injuries started telling me they saw themselves onscreen and finally felt understood and validated for their invisible disabilities. Family members and speech therapists said I got the portrayal just right. (I always thought that was funny, since we weren't really acting. We were showing how darn hard it is to cook, pay attention, stay calm, be nice, and keep on topic.)

Bill and I had just as much trouble rehearsing as we had with cooking in real life! Excited by the support, I made a second film touching on other parts of brain injury life besides our impairments. My second comedy, "Friending with Brain Injury!" takes a hard look at loneliness, discrimination against people with invisible disabilities, and the power of peer support. It was also hard to rehearse but well worth it. With this second film, I got more feedback from brain injury survivors that what we showed onscreen accurately reflected their real lives.

In just a few years making a variety of short films, starting a web-series, and directing a feature-length documentary on artists with brain injury called "Who Am I to Stop It," I learned something very valuable about media representation. We see brain injury onscreen in two main ways: in non-fiction documentary on the news, or in fiction (usually not very good) where a character has a brain injury that causes just the right kinds of impairments to make the movie work; no more and no less.

If only we got to choose so tidily in real life! The characters are not played by people with real world brain injury experience, the movies aren't written by the brain injury community, and most people would agree that the characters aren't accurate. Yet few people seem to show much annoyance with this. As a group, do we really think we can't step in and do better?

"50 First Dates" is my favorite example of a movie that shouldn't have been made without our community's input. Lucy remembers things for a whole day and then forgets it all overnight. While this type of amnesia is sort of possible, it wouldn't look much in real life like it does in the film. All the other characters use her amnesia to lie to, trick, and manipulate her, and keep her isolated from her friends and reality. In the non-disability world, we call that abuse. But since it's a brain-damaged girl, we call it "protecting her," and the film is called comedy.

Someone with a real brain injury could have performed the role much better than Drew Barrymore. She didn't seem to get it. As for documentaries, I think we need more. I believe they should be made by people with brain injury and those who know us well, since we are the ultimate experts about our own community.

This is where you come in! If you watch movies, you can make them. We live in an amazing time for media. There are so many ways for people to make and share movies, whether you went to film school or not. I want to encourage you to give it a try.

Maybe your first film won't be a polished, slick thing that brings in millions of dollars. But most films don't, even in Hollywood. So don't set your bar there.

Set your bar here: Make a movie and share it.

Make a 6-second movie with the Vine app on an Apple, Windows, or Android mobile device.

You can film on a digital camera, computer webcam, smart phone, iPod touch, tablet, or video camera. If you have enough light in the room, your image is going to look great enough to get started. If you plan the scenes before you film them, and you stick to the plan, it won't really even need editing. (Planning is a good cognitive exercise too!)

Download a free video editor to reorder scenes and add fancy transitions. Apple computers come with iMovie, and Windows computers come with Windows Live Movie Maker. Tutorials are online so you can learn that software.

Don't forget to punch it up with sounds. Find awesome free sound effects at freesound.org and free music at freemusicarchive.org.

You can share your movie on Facebook or Instagram, for example. It's free to get your own YouTube channel or use Google Drive or Google Plus to post movies and direct anyone with internet access to watch.

YouTube lets you create closed captions on your video after you put it up. You can also write a description of the visuals below the movie, for blind people to keep up. Keep access in mind so more people can enjoy your movie.

This whole movie thing is about acknowledging that you have an important perspective to share and that you are capable of sharing it, because these things are true.

Avoiding the New neighbor

A big snow had fallen where I live in rural Massachusetts, and I headed for the quiet of nearby conservation land in the 11 degree cold. I walked to the end of our road and tramped across a field into a meadow, and from there to a little bridge across a frozen stream.

I stood on the bridge, aware that this was the first winter in many years that I had taken the time to appreciate the way the snow draped the branches and caught the bright December light. The quiet sharpened the new ringing in my ears but I felt at peace. When I headed home through the drifted snow I still felt at peace.

Then I turned the bend on our road and spotted our new neighbor shoveling snow in his driveway. For four months I'd been meaning to stop by to introduce myself and welcome him to the neighborhood, but I hadn't had a day when my brain felt good enough to do it. I obviously couldn't walk by him now without saying anything, so this simple thing had become complicated.

He didn't see me, so I quickly walked back around the bend to the corner where I stood in the cold and brooded, weighing my options. Decision-making with a brain injury is no longer an automatic process. If I pressed on, I'd have to introduce myself and apologize for my failure to welcome him. I'd have to talk.

I didn't want to talk. I never want to talk. I wasn't feeling especially friendly or, God knows, articulate. No, meeting him now would be way too complicated and fraught with embarrassment. When I stammered, I'd feel compelled to say, "Oh, that? I have a brain injury." I've found myself in too many conversational corners where I have felt compelled to explain my brain injury and have seen the uncertain look on people's faces.

I see in their eyes or hear in their voices that they are trying to decide if I am mentally handicapped or even insane. Many times when the fact of my brain injury comes up, they start talking slower and simpler, as though to a child.

I didn't want to walk around the block and approach my house from the other direction because it would require a two-mile hike through heavy snow. That wasn't what I'd signed up for when I went out for a stroll. Plus, I didn't have my cell phone to call Lynne to explain why it was taking so long to get back. I decided to wait him out. And so there I stood.

More time passed. I put too much thought into how I should act when a car drove past. Standing around by the side of the road doing nothing in the intense cold looked weird. Thinking that it might be safe to approach the bend to listen for sounds of shoveling, I got closer and then closer, still out of my new neighbor's sight. I considered the possibility that he might simply be resting from shoveling, so I listened for other sounds of his presence.

Hearing nothing, I did something brave. I rounded the bend completely and walked past the foot of his driveway in full view. It was completely, blessedly shoveled from the road to his garage. I stood appreciating his work ethic, but mostly I appreciated his absence. I was emancipated! The knot in my stomach loosened, and I was free to walk the rest of the way home without having to interact with anybody!

I checked my watch. My indecision and my dread of social interaction were so overpowering that I had stood in the cold for an hour and a half. Yet most of the time, like the other TBI survivors you'll meet, I am lonely.

What I Wish I had Known

There are so many things that I wish I had known when I first fell on that patch of ice, landing directly on my skull. The sound of the "thud" is something I will never be able to clear from my head. It is my scar, my reminder of how quickly life can change. I knew from the excruciating pain I was experiencing at the impact point on my head that it was bad, really bad. But I had no idea how much my life was about to change.

I consider myself fortunate to have found a doctor right away who specializes in head injuries and concussions. However, there are still many things I feel he could have done differently to prepare me for the unexpected roller coaster that I was just getting onto. In terms of what I was about to experience, I hadn't even buckled my proverbial seatbelt yet.

That first day I remember pretty vividly. I fell at about 8:00 AM and was at the doctor's office by 10:00 AM. He checked me over and stated that I had a severe concussion and had torn a few muscles in my neck, throat, and chest. Oddly, I didn't feel any pain other than the piercing knife stabbing into my skull. It hadn't even occurred to me yet that I had other physical injuries. It was actually almost two full days before the pain set in, and then it felt like I had been run over by a truck.

I noticed many cognitive deficiencies right away. I was told that this was "normal" and I should start to see improvement in 6-8 weeks. So as I neared the end of the eighth week I was starting to panic. "What's wrong with me? Why am I not getting better? Is there something seriously wrong?" I was experiencing a lot of confusion, and I was having a lot of trouble finding the word I was looking for, and you could hear in my speech that it was taking longer to complete sentences than it should.

My doctor finally sent me to a Neurologist, who ordered an MRI to rule out anything severe. It wasn't until this point that anyone started talking about TBI. Even then, I was told it could take a few months to improve, and then not until the six month mark was I told it could take up to a year or longer.

What I wish more than anything was that my doctors had been more forthcoming with me. I understand that every brain injury is different, and not everyone will suffer the same symptoms and time frames. However, in hindsight, it is pretty clear to me that a short six to eight weeks isn't a realistic timeline. I have no doubt in my doctor's abilities, and I know he was trying to do me a "favor" by telling me I'd be fine in no time. But the truth is, I think he was damaging my recovery efforts by doing so.

I wish I had been sent to an occupational therapist right away. The neurologist brought it up, but nothing ever came of it. I wasn't in a proper state of mind to advocate for my health in the way that I normally would. I didn't have a caregiver or spouse living with me that could advocate either. I was all alone in my journey.

When I reached the six month mark of my recovery, my vertigo and balance issues increased. I started having anxiety because I didn't know what was wrong with me. I was worried that I should be getting better because that is what the doctor had said. I was thrown into a very dark, lonely place. I was starting to become depressed, something that I wasn't familiar with. I knew I was depressed, yet I didn't know what to do about it. I had no one in my support system to turn to. I felt very isolated and alone.

This cycle of despair went on for about three or four months before I had a complete and total panic attack. I honestly thought I was having a heart attack. My heart was racing, my body felt like it was floating, I wanted to cry and scream, but I had no idea why. Fortunately a dear friend was home and helped me calm down. She knew what was happening, as she had experienced panic attacks herself. I was left feeling shaken and scared. "What is wrong with me?" I kept thinking.

The next day I spoke to my doctor about what had happened. He assured me that this was "normal" and part of the recovery process. He was expecting it, as he knew that it would eventually happen to me, and was surprised it had taken me this long to have one. This was yet another thing I wish I had known about, it would have saved me from the deep sense of fear I had been feeling during the panic attack. Fortunately since that night, I have not had another attack. I have occasions where I feel the anxiety creeping up, but I am now able to fight it off with deep breathing and meditation.

It has been well over a year since my fall, and I am just NOW starting physical therapy for my injuries and occupational therapy for my cognitive issues. I feel like I am late to the party; I should have been here months ago. Late is better than never, but I have never been one to be fashionably late.

There are so many other things I wish I had known in the beginning, the list could go on and on. I realize that our doctors can't predict the future or know exactly what is happening inside our brains. Again, I feel blessed to have found a doctor right away who understood concussions and TBI. My wish is that more doctors would begin to understand the true complexity of TBI, no matter how seemingly innocent the injury appears at first. Patients and caregivers value and appreciate knowing the "worst case scenario" so that they have something to strive for (not being "worse case") and can feel like a warrior when they come out on top!

Ten Things Brain Injured Patients Want their Doctor to Know

I am writing to you today because I will be seeing you very soon for an appointment. Or perhaps I just saw you, and the appointment didn't go so well for me. Maybe this list will help you with the next brain injured patient you see. Maybe your patients' files should all indicate whether or not there is brain injury, as well as hearing or vision impairment.

I thought it would be important to share where I am coming from before you step into the examination room, and what I have learned works and doesn't work for me.

1) I am a brain injury survivor, therefore, there are things to consider about how best to conduct the appointment to make it truly beneficial. I will probably have someone with me, if at all possible, to help me remember what went on, and how to help me at home with regard to what was said.

2) Your fluorescent lights are going to trigger all kinds of bad stuff. Please understand that I need to be wearing sunglasses or a cap, or both. If you can't turn the lights off, I'll try to remember my sunglasses! And maybe if there are windows or a lamp in the room, we can just use their light while talking after the examination. I know you need the bright lights sometimes.

3) Please talk to me in softer tones unless I happen to be hard of hearing. The brain injury has caused me to have light and sound sensitivity as time has passed.

4) Please don't be in a hurry to dispense a lot of information. It is difficult to process information coming at me too quickly. That is a newer development/deficit due to the brain injury and possibly from the effect of medications. Simple, quiet questions are usually best.

5) Whatever you find to be very important for me to remember, please write it down for me, or give me time as you are talking so I can write it down. It might be a longer appointment because of that, but it is the nature of brain injury. I may have memory impairment issues (short-term, specifically). In fact, if you ask me to repeat what you just said, you'll find out how well I grasped what you said. So, you might not want to use too many big medical school terms. I might even bring a voice recorder to help me remember in the future what you said during our appointment. Thanks for understanding.

6) If I am in your office because of pain today, please don't talk at me for several minutes as we get started. Instead, please listen, and don't rush to jump in. It is difficult at times (especially when I'm tired) to compose and deliver my thoughts to you. On the flip side, please forgive me if I say them quickly and frantically - it's probably because I may be so overwhelmed by what I'm dealing with, and because I may forget what I have to say if I don't let it all out in one fell swoop....and

because it's been building up in me for two months or more since I scheduled this appointment.

7) Please do all you can to scope out my emotional well-being as we talk, and realize that most of it is due to the daily difficulties of living with the results of a brain injury, along with the daily cocktail of medicines I've been consuming perhaps for years. I may or may not be in need of anti-depressants, but I will surely be depressed if my doctor gives no indication that he's interested in how all this is impacting me.

8) Please check on what I regularly eat by asking me. It's possible that my medicines and sickness are not the only culprits besides my brain injury responsible for my symptoms today.

9) Watch for physical cues that I'm getting fatigued as we talk. I might put my head on your desk, or lie down on the table. I might cover my eyes or begin to look down. I might even get teary. You see, all of the talking and sharing of information has fatigued me to the point of mental exhaustion. The nature of the information has overwhelmed and maybe upset me. And to top it all off, I may have done other things - including traveling to the appointment - which have zapped my mental energy. It's amazing the amount of decisions my brain had to make before I stepped into your office, or the visual and aural stimulations which may have already stressed my brain and emotions.

10) Please walk with me the short way back to the front desk (or have the nurse help me) so I don't have to

remember how to re-trace my steps. You'd be surprised how confusing that path back to the waiting room might be to someone who just shot their mental wad in your exam room. And if I had to come by myself today, I'm gonna need all the help I can get.

Four Pins and a Plate

I had just finished writing an article for the Red Deer Advocate about local athlete Austin McGrath's brush with death, and subsequent miracle recovery. I did the final edit, and pressed the send button.

The article was emotionally charged and difficult to write. I needed to decompress, so I got on my bike to take the dog for a run, and in a strange twist of fate, one hour later, I was the one in the hospital, exactly two months after McGrath's May 13, 2011, cardiac arrest.

My dog Dimitri, a one year old giant schnauzer, and I were heading downhill on the Sunnybrook paths. I was going about as fast as my 52 year-old legs could go, when at the bottom of the hill my 90-pound puppy looked at me, and decided it would be a good idea to tackle his buddy.

Right away my adrenaline kicked in. I barely got the "no" out of my mouth before he collided with the bike. With my mind racing, I decided I had two choices: hit the trees (and risk getting a broken neck or back), or take my chances with the pavement. I yanked the bike back hard, hit the brakes, and went flying over the top of my bike. I bounced my forehead off of the pavement. Knowing that if my head tucked I would probably break my neck, I strained to keep it upright and in doing so watched my left wrist shatter before my eyes. I got another adrenaline rush, tucked my arm, rolled and injured my shoulder and neck, and again hit the pavement with my helmeted head.

Somehow I landed half upright 20 feet down the path from my dog and bike. For about two or three minutes I wandered around in a daze cradling my arm, indecisive, not knowing what to do. Luckily, another biker came around the corner, and asked if I needed help. It seemed to take me forever to formulate what form that help could take but finally, I handed him my cell phone and asked if he could call my wife, something I could have done myself.

With the help of the stranger, I made it to the top of the paths where we met my wife, Debbie. As I got into the passenger seat I told Debbie I thought my wrist was broken and she said, "Your helmet is pretty scuffed up too." But it was lost in the pain of my wrist.

We got to the hospital, and my wrist, which was off-centered to the left and flat as a pancake, was the focus of attention. I was asked once by a nurse how my head was and I said fine, again dealing more with the pain in my arm than anything else. Through the next two days and seeing four different doctors, no one checked me for a concussion.

Four pins, a plate, and two days later I was released from the hospital. That is when I began to have post-concussion symptoms.

My eyes were light sensitive. I was having memory recall issues, especially with people, places and things.

I was having trouble with my balance and every time I threw the dog toys they would hook left. But again all of this was lost in the pain of my wrist. Four weeks later I had my second incident. I was walking the dog down at Kin Canyon. It was a hot day, so I took Dimitri over to the fountain to drink from one of the spouts, when a little boy exploded out of the water, roaring at my dog like a dinosaur.

Dimitri startled, took off, and took my legs right out from under me. I landed with all of my weight on my forehead and my cast. I think I was out for about twenty seconds. When I came to, I was embarrassed; I spit the debris out of my mouth, dusted the dirt and grass off of my forehead and with as much dignity as possible carried on down the path.

That is when I marveled at a change in my left thumb. After the initial injury, I had very little feeling in my thumb. After my second fall, 90% of that feeling had returned. However after that second fall things got considerably more difficult for me. I quit sleeping. I am usually a nine hours a night sleeper. I went down to five then to three and then quit sleeping altogether. Along with the sleep deprivation came adrenaline, panic, and anxiety like I had never experienced before. Two days after my second accident I blacked out while walking the dog at Three Mile Bend. I was at the top of the path and then voila, somehow I was transported 100 meters further. It was the weirdest sensation, like using the transporter on Star Trek.

At the end of two weeks of not sleeping I would have said or done anything to get relief. I can now see why they use sleep deprivation as a form of torture. The smallest stressors, hunger, loud noises, stress at home would trigger full-fledged panic attacks. I became extremely noise, light, and temperature sensitive. My adrenaline was flowing all the time. I would get startle responses at the slightest sound or movement. I could no longer watch TV, listen to music, read a book, and work on the computer. My ability to focus was extremely limited. All of the above caused sensory overload. I just could not attend to anything even slightly complex.

In two small strokes of a brush I lost everything I was; father, teacher, husband, administrator, academic counsellor, athlete, coach, freelance writer; it was all gone. I was barely surviving.

Any physical activity would trigger uncontrollable migraines that would last days and weeks and even months. The migraines would start with a sore neck and numbness in my lips and nose and then move all the way down my arms and legs and then I would get a severe pounding headache and accompanying anxiety.

My balance was off. My spatial awareness was completely gone. I would hit my head all of the time, from getting into the car, to getting a box of Kleenex out of the closet. I was constantly cutting my fingers when I tried to prepare something to eat. I put plastic dishes in the oven to reheat things. Not a good idea.

Prior to the accident I was a level three boxing coach. I had my athletic training first aid certificate, but my thinking was so befuddled that I didn't even know that I had a concussion.

My thought processes were muddied. I was in a constant brain fog. My impulse control was out-of-whack, and words and thoughts would come unbidden out of my mouth. I would mix up words when I talked, sometimes substituting totally unrelated words in my sentences. It was like all of my sentences ended up in a multiple choice, and sometimes the wrong choices would just pop out.

My hearing was so sensitive I would wear sound dampening headphones, be talking on the phone and overhear word-for-word conversations and TV dialogue, two rooms over through a closed door. It was overwhelming. I joked with my family that I had superhero hearing. I had a constant ringing in my ears.

When I wore my glasses I noticed that I couldn't see properly out of my left eye. I thought I had damaged the occipital region of my brain, but when I went to the optometrist the vision in my left eye instead of getting worse had actually improved two levels.

I have been pretty active in my lifetime. I have fractured my ankle, partially torn my Achilles tendon, severed my left ACL and torn the cartilage, fractured too many ribs to count, torn my right rotator cuff twice, fractured my wrist, and fractured my nose. None of those injuries compared to the agony I felt at the height of my sleep deprivation and anxiety.

If someone had offered me another broken wrist or another torn Achilles tendon in exchange for relief from my agony, I would have taken it. I would experience all of the other injuries combined if it meant not having to face another concussive event.

When you break a wrist you have some control on how fast you heal: how hard you work in physiotherapy. When you injure your brain the biggest frustration is that lack of control. I wouldn't wish it on anyone. When you injure your wrist you have the scars and cast, when you injure your brain the scars quite often are just inside.

Being active also resulted in prior concussive events. My neurologist, Dr. Jennifer Bestard, who figured out that I had a concussion, traced back my medical history and calculated that my last two mild traumatic brain injuries were the ninth and tenth concussive events of my life. She told me that my post-concussion syndrome was the worst she had seen in her career. An MRI showed that I had bruising in eight different areas of my brain.

I had no way to describe to anyone how I was feeling. One of my former students, boxer Roman Rzepkowski, described it best when he said it was like having the worst hangover of your life, 24/7, every second, and every minute of every day.

Recovery was slow and counterintuitive to any previous injury recovery that I had experienced. Eight months after my last concussion I started back to work on a voluntary basis.

Now three years from my last head trauma, I am doing much better. I am working three quarters time. I still have some lingering symptoms, but I feel like I am functioning at about 90 to 95%. I am blessed to have had an amazing medical team that helped me put the pieces back together again.

Positives have arisen from my accident. After having my slate wiped clean, I have been given an opportunity to build a better me. I used to be the typical North American, go-go-go, 24-7. Life has slowed down. I am taking time to smell the flowers, watch the clouds, and live life in the moment.

It has also given me the opportunity to work with and help 20 different teenagers who have suffered mild traumatic brain injuries. I will continue to chronicle the obstacles, hurtles, and successes toward recovery.

Living a Purpose-Filled Life

When I was younger I had no idea what it meant to live a purpose-filled life. I wasn't a stranger to bad choices. They seemed to be something I learned at a young age and carried through to my adulthood.

Being the life of the party and having fun was my goal, even at the cost of a job, a marriage, and my self-respect. That stuff didn't matter. I was having fun and that's ALL that mattered.

Then I met John and my world started making sense. Loving someone and being loved by someone was wonderful. He didn't judge me and wanted to help me love myself and others. I was determined not to mess this up with my partying.

Despite my better choices, our lives were permanently changed on June 12, 1999 in Ogden, Utah when we were hit by a drunk driver. There were 24 shards of skull and debris driven into my brain and massive amounts of blood flowing into my brain blowing it up like a balloon. The trauma surgeon told my family, if I did wake from my coma I may be a vegetable for the remainder of my life. He stated an injury as severe as mine has a 97% mortality rate.

A miracle ensued. I spent four days in a coma and two weeks in ICU. When stable, I was flown via medical jet back home to Portland, Oregon for a month of intensive in-patient rehab at The Rehabilitation Institute of Oregon, at Good Samaritan Hospital. I went from learning to walk, talk, feeding myself and swallowing, combing my hair, and brushing my teeth, to re-learning the names of my family including my husband.

I didn't quite understand what all the fuss was about though. I was just in a car wreck. People are in wrecks every day and they simply rehab back. This was no different. And what's all this brain injury stuff they keep talking about? And why do they keep asking me the same questions over and over?

With my head shaved and a big indentation on the right side, sporting a walker for balance and wearing a helmet, after a month they let me go home. Finally things could get back to normal. I was glad I was able to convince them nothing was wrong, minus a few 'bumps & bruises.'

Over the next few months, I began to realize my injuries were more extensive than I first thought. With the help of a great psychologist who specialized in brain injury, I was able to understand the magnitude of my injuries. I wasn't going crazy because I couldn't remember things or forgot what I was saying right in the middle of a sentence, or had inappropriate outbursts of tears or anger at times. He reassured me it was the brain injury; it was that big and would try to control my life, however I could fight back. It would take rest, and lots of it - taking baby steps to find my new normal. However he assured me it could be done if I was up for the challenge and he'd be there for me.

Little by little I found my new path. I started volunteering at Good Samaritan Hospital. That led me to talking with other brain injury survivors and their families about the road back. It's tough but can be done if they surround themselves with positive, likeminded people who have their best interest at heart. Despite a brain injury they are still a WHOLE person who deserves validation and can accomplish anything they set their minds to; it simply takes re-structuring.

That re-structuring led me to co-founding a survivor-led non-profit called BIRRDsong. With our outreach continually growing we are now Brain Injury Connections NW or BIC-NW.

I started speaking in schools and on Victim Impact Panels about the ramifications of drinking & driving. However I was still feeling lost and it seemed like my message wasn't getting through.

In August of 2003, John & I flew to Arizona to attend another leadership conference to hear one of our favorite speakers, Chuck Goetschel. It was through Chuck's influence I discovered how to live a purpose-filled life. He spoke of following your dream, discovering your purpose and pursuing it with passion. I realized in that moment, that was why I survived the crash that should have killed me or left me in a vegetative state. It was to help people see their value no matter what life had dealt them. This was my purpose!

Everything we do in life begins with a choice. You choose to be a victim or a champion. You can take past mistakes and dwell on them or learn from them to teach and influence others. You can turn your tragedies into triumphs, your misery into your ministry. Without even realizing it, that's what I had done with BIRRDsong and now I could touch and save more lives!

People have a choice in how their life turns out and don't have to sit around and wait for things to happen. Attitude is altitude and in spite of mistakes, or physical or mental setbacks, a person can still go on to be a fruitful member of society. I'd learned what it meant to live a purpose filled life!

A Glimpse into my TBI

Slowly regaining consciousness, the altered vision my eyes conveys feels more like a dream than reality.

As I stare through the paned-glass window, I look over a secluded parking lot, enclosed by enormous black columns. Making a conscious effort, my eyes slowly move to the right of the window. An abundance of cards hangs on the wall, bringing the pale-cream wall to life. I am experiencing life for the first time, seeing the world through infant eyes.

I sluggishly turn my head and see my mother. Anxiety distorts her face. Almost comical. She hugs the wall with her back, rigidly standing as if to prevent herself from falling forward.

A teenage boy hovers over me. Sobbing, crying and talking, his words are muffled. I am empty - who is this? What does he mean? He never meant for this to happen!

Tension enters my body. My left arm draws inward in agitation. The heavy cast hits my chest and cuts off the circulation at my elbow. Confined to the bed, I close my eyes, silent, completely detached from the dilemma that is now my life.

It has been over 24 years since the car accident on a back road in Hampton Township, PA. At the age of 16, I was a passenger in a one-car accident. Even though

I was wearing a seatbelt, I sustained a severe traumatic brain injury (TBI). My brainstem, the delicate neurological component responsible for life sustaining processes, twisted and stretched, causing the right hemisphere of my brain to hit the inside of my skull. I immediately went into coma and was found seizing at the scene of the accident. I was Life-Flighted to Allegheny General Hospital. The doctors' prognosis was not encouraging; I would be bedridden for life and there was not much chance of any significant recovery. I was comatose for over four weeks.

It was only after I regained consciousness that the doctors changed their initial prognosis. Their story now was that it was highly unlikely that I would graduate from high school without major assistance—and higher education was out of the question. This is something my parents never told me as they did not want to discourage me from being me. I had been a 4.0 student prior to my injury; a student who tried to excel in everything she did.

As I soon learned, the cognitive issues caused by the TBI were the least of my worries. The neurological damage from my TBI resulted in numerous physical impairments. I couldn't walk; the left side of my body was severely impaired and I couldn't even hold up my head. It wobbled like a newborn's.

However, the most psychologically draining impairment was my inability to speak, eat, or drink. My tongue lay paralyzed in my mouth. The innate ability to communicate thoughts, emotions and simple daily life experiences was taken from me in a matter of seconds.

A person never consciously thinks about how words are formed and how intricate the process of speaking really is. We unconsciously vocalize thoughts: tongues instinctively move and articulate; vocal cords vibrate with sufficient breath support, combining sounds and syllables, forming words into coherent sentences. My first attempt at speaking, however, wasn't as effortless. Rational thoughts accumulated in my mind, eventually leading me to verbally express myself, but the only sound I was capable of producing was an incoherent, monotone noise. Only vocalized air, no articulation.

Regardless of whether or not anyone could understand what I was saying, I spoke indifferent to my incoherency. The thoughts in my head were clear. I knew what I was saying. Unfortunately, my audience did not have insight to the words in my mind.

It takes me quite a while to actually finish eating. I get too tired and too frustrated and am not able to finish the meal. Even though the food is placed directly on top of my teeth, it is difficult to actually move the food around in my mouth. I need to use the nook to move it back over my teeth to chew. My swallowing reflex is getting stronger day-by-day, however, moving the food around in my mouth with my tongue is another thing. My tongue barely moves.

I do not remember anyone ever telling me that I had been in a car accident and that I had sustained a severe TBI. I don't remember anyone ever telling me the life I had lived for 16 years was now over, or that I would have to rebuild a life for myself. I had to learn this for myself, piece by piece, bit by bit.

I felt like a child who was learning everything for the first time, but I knew I would get better, it would just take time. There has been a light behind my continuing desire and determination to succeed and it keeps me going day by day. I will always push myself. I have learned to overcome most of my physical impairments, including speech. I do not have my old, pre-injury voice back, but I do speak intelligibly now and most strangers I meet do not have trouble understanding me.

Despite doctors' prognosis, I did graduate high school in the top 10% of my class. I also went on to higher education. I have a BA in Sociology from West Virginia Wesleyan College and two Masters Degrees - one in Literary and Professional Writing from DePaul University and one in Transition Special Education with emphasis in acquired brain injury from The George Washington University (GWU).

I also have an Ed.D. from GWU in Special Education with a concentration in brain injury and am a Certified Brain Injury Specialist (CBIS). My personal, educational and professional endeavors have been focused on the field of ABI. I am a brain injury education specialist and started ABI Education Services, LLC a business that provides consultation, training, transition services and in-school support for children, adolescents and young adults with brain injury. I have excelled beyond everyone's expectations but my own.

Seven Schools – One Degree

It's rough having a brain injury. Like many others, I can get overwhelmed very easily. I freaked out at one school in the parking lot and never even made it to the first class, so that doesn't really count does it?

Moving forward toward getting my degree was an exhausting process. I started my first college class while I was stationed in Germany. I was pregnant with my daughter.

Unaware I had both post traumatic stress disorder (PTSD) and a traumatic brain injury, I enrolled at University of Maryland and took classes all over the country. Later that year I was kicked out of my house, only to arrive back in Massachusetts with baby Kat on Christmas Eve.

A few months later, I enrolled in an EMT course. By the end of the course, I realized it was not a good fit, so I enrolled in community college. I struggled with learning the campus, but academically did great until the mid-summer semester when my headaches were so overwhelming that I couldn't get out of bed to finish my classes.

I was taking week-long intersession courses to get caught up, but by now my GPA was suffering. I never made it to the office to properly withdraw, resulting in failing marks on my record. Trying not to be phased, I applied and was admitted into UMass Boston. My momentum soon dissipated as I completely flipped out in what I considered to be an unsafe stairwell leading up to registration.

I then decided to enroll in a couple classes at a nearby junior college, where I excelled and transferred my credits to get my Associates Degree. It was time for me to try a four year school.

I started attending UMass Dartmouth with a full course load and had huge anxiety about my safety on campus. The walk between the parking lot and my night classes was heavily treed. Campus news about the high rape incidents really freaked me out. I began getting migraines and my PTSD spiked to the point I couldn't go to class.

At the time I had no diagnosis or knowledge of what was going on, and really began to hate myself for failing. I tried again at summer session, but then had a professor from the school asking me out and calling me at home.

This really stressed me and I dropped all my classes once again. I was working third shift loading trucks for the Teamsters at this time so I could spend time with my daughter during the day. With little sleep, my TBI symptoms escalated.

Over the next few years I took a class here and there and at different community colleges. On the verge of losing my GI Bill benefits (the military scholarship I sacrificed so much for), I decided to go back to school full-time and leave my job at the Waldorf School. I just couldn't stand working for the low wages they offered and really wanted a few letters after my name. This didn't go over well with my husband at the time and we eventually divorced. I became even more committed to finishing my degree now that my daughters relied on me more heavily than ever.

I missed BSU fall applications but was able to enroll in full-time courses anyway. During winter break I got a denial letter for admissions, though I was at the top of my classes. After talking with an admissions rep, she stated it was because I dropped out of classes at my last two degree-seeking schools. I was told that the only way I could get around that was to go back to one of them and successfully complete a course.

That semester, in addition to three classes at BSU, I re-enrolled in a degree program at Massasoit and took a single class. It worked and I was accepted to BSU. I spent a full year at BSU without being a matriculated student, which meant no financial aid, no loans, and all debt on my credit card. I felt I had to do whatever it took, and I did.

After a total of ten years and several different schools, I completed my Bachelorette in Science in Accounting and Finance, with a concentration in Accounting. Additionally, I was named BSU student of the week at one point. I had so much momentum built up that I took my GMAT without even having taking the suggested classes for the test, passed, and enrolled in Graduate School.

Receiving special permission to enroll in more courses than allowed, I then finished my Master's Degree in just one year. Now nineteen years later and just learning of my diagnoses, I can't believe I did it all without any help from Student Special Services.

Going through a divorce and moving a few times, I had multiple physical hurdles, including surgery. Being a single parent with no family support and hours of commute time each day, I was able to graduate amid a long list of insanities that were present in my life at that time.

Looking back, I now consider going to school to be one of my strong suits. Yes, it's challenging having a need to always sit in the back corner. Now I can look back and smile. I've rewritten my educational history to be successful. However, I'm also not ready to stop here. The future now has limitless possibilities!

Living in a War Zone

After a trauma, an illness or an addiction, life becomes an uphill battle in all situations. Whether it's dealing with doctors, drug companies, mental health and rehabilitation professionals, or any other support staff, living as an independent, self-sufficient human being is simply no longer possible. There are countless adjustments, accommodations and modifications that need to be made to ensure the possibility that a quality life will be realized.

Now, let's bust some myths about living with challenges: First, true independence is simply no longer a possibility. Total dependence on anything is undesirable. A mixture of both independence or self-sufficiency, and dependence or getting assistance when needed becomes your new normal. Being interdependent with the environment becomes a new success strategy. Not over-using available support shows strength as you make progress and achieve new goals.

It's important to remember that behavior after tragedy is often fleeting and needing reminders of directions is not unusual or a cause for concern. Having memory problems is simply your new way of being. This document is for all those who've lost something and wonder if they will ever regain a life worth living.

It is also for people who haven't experienced a life altering calamity and want to know what that feels like. After existence as you had known it has ended, you must fight your way back! I make that statement because it's simply the absolute truth – for everybody! Regardless of the injury, disability, illness or addiction, that's just the way it is.

Since sustaining a severe closed head/brain stem injury in 1971, I've had more than my share of medical and psychological problems. I'm as healthy as I can be for a brain injured person. I address my difficulties as they arise. I see lots of specialists and I undergo medical procedures all the time. I have problems with my balance, my memory, and the organization of my days. I have to write down everything that I want to do and remember. I keep two calendars. One is in my kitchen near the telephone and the other I carry with me wherever I go. My cell phone isn't a smart one, because I know that I wouldn't remember how to use it. I take public transportation because I've lost my driving privileges due to excessive speed and poor decision making.

I don't work because I'm never sure which days will be good ones and I'll be able to do what I want, the way I want, and which days are ones that I shouldn't have left the house. Oh well - that's my life in a nutshell. It's not pretty, but I make it work for me!

With any wound, it takes time to recover. Things never seem to get back to just the way they were. Typically, this is when depression rears its ugly head. When the realization that you just can't do things the way you used to becomes a reality, then a choice has to be made by you, the survivor. Do you give up and stop trying or do you fight the long battle back? It's your choice. No one can decide for you, not your significant other or your parent, employer, doctor or commanding officer. They can help you on your journey back to health and well-being, but they can't do what needs to be done. Only you can! So, what do you do?

I'll tell you what I do. I accept what is, because I have to. I don't have the luxury of having multiple choices. Then, I find the good in my situation and I forgive all those who I think may have hurt me. My attitude is that I will not let my circumstances control me. I will make adjustments in how I live, so that I can have the life that I want. It's really that simple!

Creating Success in our Lives

Life changes when you experience a brain injury: those of us who have experienced a TBI know this better than anyone else. Life becomes a crazy, mixed up jumble, where everything has changed…except for one thing.

That one thing that doesn't seem to change is our expectations: our expectations about what we should be able to do, as well as how we should be able to function as human beings.

A brain injury is sudden and cataclysmic. After experiencing a TBI, we are forced to go through a learning period where we attempt to come to grips with the changes that have occurred. That takes time. There are so many changes that it literally takes years for us to understand exactly what our capabilities are. Not until we understand our capabilities, can we adjust our expectations.

Learning about ourselves and adjusting our expectations is crucial to creating success.

Many of us feel that changing our expectations is the same as throwing in the towel and giving up. Of course, no one wants to surrender, and we need to realize that changing our expectations is not the same as giving up. Rather, we are adapting to our new circumstances. We are learning what it takes to thrive in a new world.

Much of our self-worth and happiness is based on how we, as human beings, relate to and fulfill those expectations. When our capabilities change due to TBI and our expectations do not adjust, we are setting ourselves up for repeated failure. Basically, we are stuck in an old reality, and we constantly beat ourselves up and get down on ourselves for not being able to do something we have always been able to do.

Some of the most debilitating effects of brain injury are the negative feelings that we develop about ourselves, and how these feelings and thoughts affect what we do. However, how we feel about ourselves is driven by our expectations, and thus, is something we can control.

Yes, while we may not be in complete control of our capabilities, we are in control of our expectations.

The equation is simple: In order to feel more successful I would need more successes, and in order to have more successes I'd have to change my expectations of what success is for me. I need to adjust so I am not beating myself up so much.

We spend years getting to know ourselves and creating expectations of ourselves. These expectations come naturally when we see how we function in situations, and we take pride in being able to perform and fulfill our expectations.

The knowledge we have gained over the years is thrown away in a split second by brain injury, and rebuilding that knowledge base is difficult. No one wants to chuck aside all their life experiences, as well as all the work they have invested in themselves – the work that has created the expectations they have – and start anew.

Our pride is involved. Our ego too. We find it difficult to give up what we knew about ourselves, but the reality is we have changed, and we are asking our expectations, based on what we have learned about ourselves, to change. It is important to understand that creating a culture of success has less to do with what we do and more to do with our expectations.

We are facing some period of time where we are getting to know our new "selves". It's not always easy to adjust our expectations. We have to go through a lot of trials and failures in order to learn about ourselves. And you have to put your ego aside so that you can accept your new expectations.

If we don't adapt and learn we will be trapped in a cycle of failure. We want to build a culture of success, where we understand our capabilities and we build our expectations around what is possible.

Finding a way to be successful in life after TBI is so very important. It can also be scary. Anything that involves risk and change can be scary. In fact, we may even be more comfortable keeping our old expectations, knowing we will continue to fail, rather than to take risks and try to be successful.

Changing your expectations doesn't mean giving up dreams and aspirations, but it may mean changing them or re-examining them in order to either make them come true, make some semblance of them come true, or make something else happen.

The goal here is not to beat ourselves up all the time, either for things we can't do that we think we should be able to, or for ways that other people act towards us. The ultimate goal should be to feel successful and productive, and we can start by making a very personal choice to change the expectations we measure success against so they are realistic and attainable.

I am a Miracle

My life forever changed Christmas night of 2009. My mind, body and soul were different. I dropped my four girls off with their dad when we were done having Christmas brunch with my parents, said my good-byes, gave them kisses and left. I went to a birthday party for someone I worked with, 45 minutes north.

I had a blast! I laughed and drank alcohol, then decided around 10:30 pm to go home. I gave hugs to the people at the party, said my good-byes and they asked, "Are you okay to drive home?" "Totally," I said, and assured them I was fine and left. Heading north on the 57 freeway, I was confused and lost so I called a close friend for directions.

He could tell I was drunk and told me to pull over and he would pick me up. I didn't listen and while arguing with him, I rolled down an embankment onto the 60 freeway just below the freeway I was just on! I hit alternator sand barrels which stopped my car; I hit no one else but was trapped in my car unconscious. While knocked out, in a coma, I spoke to the Spirit of God; I felt incredible peace and love. He said He is going to take care of me, not to worry, just rest in Him. Sadly, people passed my crashed vehicle on the side of the road without stopping to check to see if I was okay; close to 11 pm, about 20 minutes after the accident happened, someone stopped to try and help me out. When he couldn't, he called 911.

The paramedics came within minutes and had to use the Jaws of Life to cut the car open and get me out. Not knowing where to take me, UCI or UCLA either by ambulance or helicopter, they decided to take me to UCI by ambulance. I wasn't breathing well and broken in several places including the shattering of my face and right arm; I was assessed in the ambulance, my breathing was short. I was considered Ring Jane Doe when taken to UCI because I was wearing a wedding ring but still needed to be identified. Jesus was with me every moment.

After UCI assessed me, they concluded I suffered a traumatic brain injury (TBI). My friend, whom I was speaking with when the accident happened, called my apartment and several hospitals to see if he could find me because our talk was cut off when the accident occurred. Once he called UCI, they told him a woman was brought in but they did not know who I was, so he had to go to the hospital to verify I was the person on my driver's license; this was the evening after Christmas.

He called my sister to let her know I was in an accident and in the hospital. She then called my parents and they came to the hospital to see what state I was in. I was given a 38% chance of living. The first three days were most crucial for my survival; I had two surgeries. The first surgery was to fix my head and my face. I had six plates and some metal screws put into my face and my jaw was wired shut. The second surgery was to work on my very broken right arm; a long plate was put in place of the shattered bone.

Through all of this, I nestled in the Lord's presence while in my coma; He kept telling me He loved me; He is taking care of me; He has big things in store; trust and rely on Him and never, never give up!

I was in a coma for two and a half weeks, and then my eyes began to slowly open. Once somewhat awake, UCI transferred me to a rehab hospital in Brea named Kindred Hospital. I had to relearn EVERYTHING like how to walk and talk again, how to eat food, even how to use the bathroom! I was a quick learner; my spirit wanted me to improve.

I was discharged from Kindred on St. Patrick's Day, March 17, 2010. I was unclear about so much, but I listened and trusted the people helping me, plus the Spirit of God was with me encouraging me. I moved in with my mom and dad because I was separated from my husband, he did not want me to live with him and the kids. But I received many visits from my four girls. My mom picked them up or their dad dropped them off; they needed to see their mom they almost lost and I needed to be around them to help my memories come back.

After coming home with my parents, my mom drove me to Winways, a place to relearn for people with brain injuries. I received many therapies five days a week for two months. Due to the problems with my perception and not knowing much, it was recommended that I go to Coastline Community College, a program that focused on different strategies following an acquired brain injury. It also was recommended I continue hand therapy so I could bend and move my fingers, and that I continue outpatient speech therapy so I wouldn't slur my words or often repeat myself.

I began Coastline College on June 21, 2010 (my 32nd birthday). Although I wasn't completely together in my mind, my spirit and my soul wanted improvement and I wanted what was lost! I went to the 'brain-school' four days a week, four hours a day, for two years. OCTA (transportation service) took me every day until I got my license reinstated two months before finishing Coastline College in 2012. Jesus was with me every step of the way! And just like He told me in my coma, He was and is taking care of me, do not worry! I honestly do not get through my days without His help and guidance; He saved me for a purpose! I AM A MIRACLE!

My Experience with Brain Injury

I open my eyes and I have no idea where I am. Am I dreaming? My Aunt and Uncle are standing over me. I reach out and grip my Uncle's hand as tightly as I can. I can't let go. Looking down, my brand new jersey is ripped open. Soccer boots on my feet, socks, shin guards still on. Wires are stuck all over my chest and there is a tube in my nose. I can hear machines beeping behind me. Slowly it dawns on me something must have happened. I am in a hospital bed. "You had an accident at soccer," my Aunt says.

That's the most I can remember of waking up that day, March 18th, 2013. I have no memory of what occurred several hours prior, but now I know that it has changed my life forever. It was the first game of the season for my soccer club, Kangaroo Point Rovers, and I was the Goalkeeper. My team had trained hard in pre-season and was confident of mounting a challenge for the grand finale. What follows is an account of the events, as told to me by others who witnessed them. In the third minute of the game, the ball fell between an opponent and I, both sprinting at full pace to try and get to it first. I dived at his feet to try and get my hands onto the ball, and just beat him to it.

As his momentum carried on, he tried to hurdle over me but his knee struck the left side of my head, just above the temple. My head snapped backwards. Players from both teams looked on, not knowing what to do as I went into a seizure. My limbs jerked, my eyes rolled back and I foamed at the mouth. Fortunately, a team mate that day was an off duty ambulance paramedic and knew what to do and gave me immediate care. I often wonder what might have been had he not been there. Completely unconscious I was rushed to the Princess Alexandra Hospital by ambulance.

I spent a few days recovering and being monitored at the PA. The Neurologists had performed a quick CT scan whilst I was unconscious. The scan revealed a minor bleed on the surface of my brain as a result of the collision. Thankfully, I was assured this was nothing to worry about and would make a full recovery. Feeling quite relieved, all I could think about was getting back onto the soccer field as soon as possible. Being out of action didn't feel like an option at this point in my life, also professionally I was really starting to gather pace and didn't want to take time off work either.

Prior to that day in March 2013, I had worked from home as a freelance draftsman and my business was really taking off. Having grown a bit weary after 13 years of employment with various engineering consultancies in the UK and Australia, I had decided to go solo and set up on my own. Relationships were being forged with clients and they were returning regularly with new projects for me to work on. Working hard and playing hard, I was one of the boys, with plenty of big drinking sessions to enjoy with my soccer mates and I was always right in the middle.

When I was discharged from hospital, it quickly became apparent to me that I didn't feel quite right, though it was hard to put my finger on it. Physically I seemed fine, and on the outside I looked normal. I was incredibly tired all of the time. Exhausted and vague. People would talk to me and I couldn't fully understand what they were saying. It was as though they were talking in a foreign language at times. Communication became a problem – I could not articulate how I felt or what I needed. The words felt as though they were on the tip of my tongue but would not come out.

Most of those around me quickly became frustrated. What is wrong with you? Why can't you tell us what is wrong? You need to snap out of it! These were regular anecdotes from a variety of people in my life. It wasn't their fault for saying these things and they wanted to help, they just didn't understand it and were very worried. Those valuable relationships with clients I had worked hard to foster ceased to exist as I became completely incompetent at my job, and my bank account dwindled. The old Grant seemed to be disappearing fast – and people were regularly telling me so, which added to a growing sense of shame and guilt. Having no idea at the time what all of this meant, I couldn't seem to get things together. Becoming increasingly isolated, I became very thin and rarely left my bedroom. I would later find out the extent of damage to my brain was far greater than first known.

Returning to the Brain Injury Rehabilitation Unit (BIRU) at the PA Hospital, I discussed my symptoms with the specialists and was given further testing. Detailed MRI scans revealed what the original quick CT scan had not picked up. I had suffered what is known as a Diffuse Axonal Injury. At the moment the opposing player's knee had collided with my head, the impact caused my brain to bounce around within my skull. This caused dozens of minor bleeds and areas of damage where the soft brain tissue made contact with bony ridges on the inside surface of my skull.

The results of Diffuse Axonal can be catastrophic. The outcome is quite often coma with most patients never regaining full consciousness – yet I had been incredibly lucky. The prognosis was very uncertain – people with even a minor brain injury can still have ongoing significant cognitive problems after six to twelve months and patients with more serious injuries can be relatively back to themselves just a few months down the line. One thing is for sure, with any injury of this type the road to recovery is uncertain.

No two brain injuries are the same. For me, a long period of rehabilitation as an outpatient followed. Every week I would attend the BIRU to try and re-train my brain to overcome and adapt to the injuries it had received. The occupational therapists showed me a book with pages of different faces and asked me to memorize a dozen or so of them. Ten minutes later, when asked which faces I had previously seen, I could not recall most of them. As a test, they asked me to go down to the hospital café and order a coffee, buy a newspaper and then return to the BIRU.

Roughly thirty minutes later the staff found me wandering around the hospital confused – I had no memory of the instructions I had been given just minutes previously. These are a couple of examples but there were countless more. This period of my life brought various emotions, fear, anger, resentment, guilt, shame. Most of all, confusion. Considering myself a fairly competent person, I found it all terrifying.

Thankfully, following a relatively successful period in rehabilitation, things slowly began to improve for me. Today I am two and a half years down the track from my brain injury. I feel like I am getting better every day but still have moments where I have to slow things down. My recovery is still ongoing. Without the support of my aunt and uncle, I wouldn't have come through it. They really were fantastic and picked me up during some tough times. I will be forever indebted to them. Many of the friends and drinking pals I had accumulated before my accident are now long gone – but the good mates have remained through thick and thin.

I decided to give up alcohol to aid my recovery, as it's toxic for the brain, especially a damaged brain. This was very difficult and took some getting used to. For fifteen years the booze had been my primary source of fun but had also taken me to some dark places and I knew I had been using it too much to cope with the stresses in my life. Having not touched a drop for 30 months now, I don't miss it at all – especially the hangovers!

I can say with all honesty that my brain injury is the best thing that has ever happened to me – and I wouldn't change it. Coming to terms with it has helped me become a better person and I have met and befriended some amazing people as a result, people I would never have crossed paths with had it not been for my accident. Participating in voluntary group work with others at the STEPS group is something I have found very rewarding.

On Monday mornings, I give my own time to assist with leading the STEPS skills program, a Queensland Health initiative which delivers support to people in the community who have suffered an ABI (acquired brain injury). Usually these car crash, stroke, fall, and other accident victims are discharged from hospital once the physical wounds have healed. Often, little is known regarding the full extent of the damage that has been caused to the brain and the person's psychological wellbeing. STEPS offers group work sessions to help them share their experiences with others and learn how to adapt and look after themselves following such life changing injuries. Having been through it all myself, I can offer advice, empathy and understanding. It has helped my recovery, and especially my mental health, immensely.

I am a big advocate of discussing mental health, especially in men. Coming from a working class English town, you are conditioned to keep your feelings bottled up. You work hard and play hard, and keep your problems to yourself. You get on with it. That's just the way it is. Having had my own battles with depression, both before and after my brain injury, I'm not ashamed to admit I have sought treatment and counselling. I found this the hardest thing to admit to myself and especially others that I needed help. I just wish more men would do it if they are struggling – suicide is the biggest killer of men between the ages of 20 and 49, not cancer or lifestyle related diseases.

Men are expected to be men, and always be strong. I'm not saying women don't suffer, of course they do, but men are more inclined to keep things bottled up and not talk about it, whereas women are more likely to. Men can often see it as detrimental to their masculinity. I think the stigma surrounding mental health is slowly improving, especially with high profile public figures and sports stars going public with their own struggles. Sadly, I feel there is still a long way to go before mental health issues are more out in the open and widely accepted.

I returned to playing soccer roughly twelve months ago, which was difficult at first but I am somewhere near back to my best again. Perhaps my reflexes are a little slower, but maybe that's just age creeping up on me! In a recent game I fractured a cheekbone, on the receiving end of an opponent's stray elbow, which shook me up a little. I have been warned by doctors that another significant head injury could be disastrous. Being fully aware of the risks, I have to be very careful, but it's a physical game and strong challenges are part of it. People often ask if I am crazy for going back onto the field but my answer is always the same, I just love the game and I'm not thinking about retiring from the game anytime soon!

Double Trauma

It's been almost three years since the knock on our door completely changed our lives forever. My husband ran downstairs first, and I heard a voice saying, "There's been a fatal accident. Your oldest son didn't survive, and his brother is in very critical condition with a severe head injury. He isn't expected to live." All I could say was, "You have the wrong house."

I waited for the police officers to leave. They didn't. When I begged to go to our oldest son, Aaron (he was 26 when he died), I remember my husband saying to me, "Norma, there is nothing we can do for Aaron, but Steven needs us. This is what Aaron would want." At the time, his truthful words made me angry, but those words ended up being a defining moment for me. Shock took over my body coupled with a determined "I will do anything I can to keep my only son alive" mentality! I spent every allowed waking moment by Steven's side, begging my 22-year-old to live.

I somehow managed to shift gears as needed to be Steven's cheerleader while making lists to ensure that Aaron's life celebration was everything he deserved. When forced to leave Steven's room, I would start checking off my "Aaron" list. There was an obituary to be written, perfect songs to be chosen, pictures to sort. Aaron's hunting trophies, including a 300-pound bear, needed to be delivered to the church. There was no time for sleep.

I felt guilty when we had to leave the hospital to go to the funeral home and was plagued with more guilt because I couldn't focus on the painful task of picking out a casket for Aaron — I was afraid Steven would die while we were at the funeral home. If humanly possible, more guilt consumed my worn-out body as I attended our son's visitation and life celebration, silently praying that Steven would live until I could get back to him. So when asked how I coped with Steven fighting for his life while trying to accept the fact that we lost our first-born son, I give credit to God for creating our bodies in such a way that allows us to operate even while in shock.

I somehow managed to compartmentalize my emotions. While Aaron was on my mind every minute, I was consumed with dread: I have to get Steven through this, he can't die, we have to get him to the best rehab, and we have to make whatever sacrifices necessary to give him the best possible chance of recovery. To be honest, it was easier to focus on Steven's recovery than to focus on the reality that Aaron died.

I found out the hard way that when faced with trauma of this magnitude, your body has many protective layers; and as the layers are slowly peeled back, you find out exactly what resiliency is. As the third-year anniversary of this horrible accident approaches, I'm living with delayed grief. I've learned first-hand what PTSD is. As our surviving son becomes more independent with each passing day, I'm left with attempting to figure out what's next for me. I have learned many lessons through counseling; one of the most valuable is accepting the reality that you can't put a time limit on grief. This is especially true when dealing with a double trauma and delayed grief.

For today, I will focus on being thankful for the years that Aaron so richly blessed our lives and cherishing each day with our miracle son Steven. While we don't know where this journey is ultimately leading us, we will continue to persevere, being thankful to God that we have each other, our family, friends, and our community!

The Brain Injury I Never Knew I Had

At the time of my motor vehicle crash in 1977, when I was 22-years-old, they didn't have a name for what happened to my head. Just blood and a flap of skin.

X-rays looked okay. Sew it up and move on to the more important things, like broken bones. Will she ever walk again?

At the time of my motor vehicle crash, I was just finishing college and was ready to take on the world. In spite of my doctor's concern about a "neurological event," I persuaded my parents to let me go to graduate school.

But they had to come rescue me at the end of the first semester, when I was confused and tired. I waited a year and then tried graduate school again. I went on to my first job, but fell apart after 3 years. I came home for a spell, and then went to graduate school again, this time in a different field: business. I managed to keep busy in three different jobs and I raised two children. But after 20 years, when the job was stressful and the children were teenagers, I fell apart completely.

It was then, 27 years after my senior year in college ended with a bang, that I went to a neuropsychologist who told me I wasn't crazy. I was just brain injured.

Jobless and middle-aged, I tried to understand what it meant to have a brain injury. I 2004, there wasn't nearly as much information on the Internet. That was still before we heard much about the signature wound of the wars in Iraq and Afghanistan or the concussion crisis in football. I was only able to find one survivor story, Claudia Osborne's book, Over My Head. I read the book. I tried to find a new job. I was barely a good parent.

Then, in 2009, when I was 54 years old, over three decades after the car crash, my father had a stroke and I had an "aha moment." I saw my cognitive communication problems mirrored in my dad's aphasia and word-finding difficulties.

I stopped and thought about how awesome it is that the brain regulates our verbal and non-verbal communication and therefore is the seat of our personality. I got so excited about the science of language I glimpsed during his therapy sessions with a speech-language pathologist that I went back to graduate school for the third time. In speech therapy, I thought I found something that would help me and others.

Unfortunately, I didn't know enough about what it meant to be a real speech-language pathologist, especially a real SLP with a brain injury. It was hard, but I was learning, so I thought.

In clinical practice, the SLP is always on her toes, listening to clients, reasoning out their speech and swallowing related difficulties, thinking about the brain functions that relate to thinking up the words that do or don't come out of their mouths.

I wanted to work with people with cognitive-communication problems, people like my father and me, who would need to learn strategies that would improve their ability to communicate successfully with others. I knew that I had not been a successful communicator because I didn't know that my problems were all in my head, in the damaged brain cells and neurochemistry!

Instead of thinking that my problems were brain based and something that could be rehabilitated, I had only gotten mad at myself for doing stupid things. I beat myself up a lot. I had emotional meltdowns and yelled at people because I thought the communication problems were their fault. I thought people weren't being nice to me. I didn't know that the problem was me.

Toward the end of graduate school I found myself working in a clinical externship with a no-nonsense supervisor. She began to point out to me that I wasn't a very good therapist. I was completely shocked! How could this be so? I was making all A's and a few B's. I was handling my emotions and working so much better in relationships with other people now that I understood aspects of my brain injury. I thought I was coping so well.

Now that I get it, I am just amazed that people with brain injury are so unaware of the affect their brain injury symptoms have on their ability to be successful in their careers and social life.

What occurred to me next was something more than an aha moment. Because I was studying the brain and working with people with brain injury, it began to wash over me that I was an example of what I was studying and that I was one of them. That trip through the windshield had taken me to the other side where my acetylcholine deficit was forever. My left side deficit was due to an incurable upper neuron injury. I knew what it meant to have permanent auditory processing delay. The legs that broke in multiple places were now full of arthritis and oh so painful.

My no-nonsense supervisor was right. I could not be a very good therapist given that I was living and aging with brain injury symptoms. These symptoms would limit my ability to perform the job of a speech-language pathologist.

At first, this realization floored me. I fell into deep depression again because I had failed to be able to do what I thought I could do.

But this time, I snapped out of it. I snapped out of it because I decided to accept that brain injury places permanent limitations. Before, I hadn't acknowledged I was limited. I had been trying to get on with the life I expected, but that darn supervisor put me in my place. She put me in my brain-injured place.

But she didn't count me down and out. She gave me a new lease on a new, right-sized life. I realized that I could push the limits if I wanted to, but that I had to make peace with the limits and not let them get me down. It took a lot of years and a lot of tears, but now I am free to be my best brain-injured self.

And now I can truly help people like my father and me. Perhaps I won't get to wear an SLP badge in a busy hospital setting, but there is nevertheless so much that I can do in other right-sized places. I work part-time as an SLP in a small, private clinic. I facilitate two brain-injury survivor support groups. I wrote my survivor story to share with the world. I advocate for greater awareness of brain injury. I've trained a therapy dog. It's okay. I'm doing my best and I finally know what that means.

Rethinking the Holidays

For many, getting through the holidays is a struggle. People have an idea in their mind of what they expect for the perfect family gatherings, traditions, parties and special dinners, as well as expectations of others they'll be spending time with. When all that is mixed together with disappointments or un-forgiveness of past behaviors of those others or ourselves, or other unresolved family issues, we can see why it is truly a difficult time for many… on a good day.

Adding any kind of illness or injury complicates things, especially if that injury carries with it long term recovery times such as brain injury. I say this about brain injury because there are so many unknowns complicating the actions and reactions of the injured person, and those around, that most times no one really knows what to expect. While everyone involved is dealing with so many uncertainties, preparing in advance is a must. Plan for and educate those who may not fully understand the situation, then do your best. Find creative ways to accomplish what needs to be done to keep you or your loved one comfortable. Simple is good.

I never thought the injuries I experienced from an auto accident were going to be long term. I thought I would be back to normal (or what was normal for me) in a week or so. Even when I was told to expect a 3-5 year recovery, I was sure they had mixed up my file with someone else's.

The first Thanksgiving came; to this day all I can tell you about it is I was there with all my children, grandchildren and a few others, nothing else. The same is true of Christmas; it came and went, I have no memory of that either. We loved and celebrated life every day in our house, but the holidays were even more so. I loved the tradition of it – my families' traditions, the colors, the lights, and especially the music. In fact you could hear Christmas music played throughout the year at my house because I loved the way it made me feel, always cheery, upbeat and hopeful. One of our traditions had been when Thanksgiving dinner was over, Christmas began. As the table was cleared, food put away, with the turkey bones picked over and on the stove for the next day's soup, the music started with Elvis Christmas. Everyone danced around the kitchen and helped – everyone!

There was so much that I didn't participate in All YEAR that first year. Because our family was so large, normally I started right after Christmas planning and shopping for the next year. By Thanksgiving I would have everything done, gifts wrapped, and filled with anticipation of the excitement and joy on the faces of those I loved when they opened their gifts. It was never quite clear who was more excited: those receiving, or me excited over giving them. While others were ramping up going through holiday rush and sales I could sit back and enjoy every minute of it. If I ran into something extra it was just icing on the cake. To miss that was huge. Huge for me because I wasn't doing it, huge – especially my husband, because he was by default doing his job and also mine. I was with my family and missing them all at the same time.

By the time the second Thanksgiving came around I was more awake. I don't remember helping much; I probably slept until everyone showed up. All my children, their children and others were all there talking, joking, and laughing. I don't remember it, with the exception of shortly into the meal I was unable to process everything, which turned to overload and shaking. I had to take my plate to another room where it was quiet for everything to calm down. Everyone knew and we all wished it was different, but until improvement came we did what needed to be done to get through.

I remember the second Christmas because we were in the process of moving. My husband, our two youngest children and I spent Christmas at the Residence Inn. We (really my husband did most of it) cooked a Christmas dinner on a much smaller scale, we had a small little tree from the floral department of a local store and we each had one gift. It was quiet and full of love and I will never forget it.

Life is always changing and we have changed with it, the holidays are no different. We like to make memories our gifts. We go places, do things, we're silly, and we laugh and play. We've gone to the balloon fiesta in New Mexico, having Christmas in October. Or we can be found celebrating at the beach in August. We plan in advance – every other year we go someplace together. That way everyone saves up for what we are to do. Even the younger grandchildren love this more so than the traditional celebrations. This is an awesome way to celebrate, especially when separated by distance – no worries about others traveling in bad weather or getting stuck in an airport or dealing with the crowds. The other thing about it is that it's a memory etched in everyone's heart and mind, unlike the sweater or toy that will go by the wayside or be forgotten in several months. We will be with our children long after we are gone through the memories we create with our time.

I consider myself healed even though I do several things differently. Because I no longer frequent places with high EMF (electro-magnetic fields) like major cities, concerts, malls, and such, my husband takes one of the kids with him to do things he would like to do that I no longer can do. This is a great thing for all of us. He never has to feel like he is missing out on something he would like to do and has one on one time bonding those relationships. When they get back I get to see and hear it through them, their excitement, their experience, so they relive it again with me. The kids also spend time with me doing other things that I never used to do, maintaining my bond with them. Even though our children are fully-grown it's important to have and maintain a good relationship with us together and each separately.

We haven't stopped there; while we do love the whole traditional dinner thing we also love Mexican food. On Thanksgiving and Christmas I fix enchiladas, fresh beans, and rice, then we do the traditional meal another day. Don't be afraid to switch things up. Adjust to what is easiest for everyone concerned so that everyone has a great time.

From Tragedy to Triumph

In a split second, the life that I once knew vanished forever. Abandoned to the whims of fate, my inner world was tossed into complete chaos. Here, emotions and feelings had no source, no rhyme or reason.

In Toronto, Canada, in 1969, on a cold and dark wintry evening, while out conducting routine business, I tumbled head first down a steep flight of stairs. After suffering a devastating head and brain injury and a near-death experience, I woke up in a hospital bed. At the foot stood three complete strangers: my husband and two young daughters. Later, looking in the bathroom mirror, I beheld the horrific image of a gargoyle.

Escaping the doctor's knife, I left my husband and absconded with my two daughters to England. There I looked to the only person I could trust: my mother. But standing in my way was a stepfather who was determined to make my life a living hell. Forced out of my mother's home while being hooked on massive doses of uppers, downers and barbiturates, I rented a house for my daughters and myself.

Sadly, even with my youngest daughter acting as caregiver it became abundantly clear I didn't possess the mental or emotional capacity to be the mother I once was. Even with sending my beloved girls back to live with their father in Canada, his stable love could not keep my children from developing emotional problems.

Suffering on the brink of madness, I lived in an incredible world on the fringes of reality. While re-experiencing infancy, adolescence and early adulthood, I made my way into English society only to become a vulnerable target for unscrupulous predators. They knew, without having to be told, that within my beautiful, mature body lived a child-like mind. But I had my protectors too in the form of well-known jazz musicians who took me under their wing.

My sixteen years of recovery were not without their humorous moments. Verbal dysphasia and comical anecdotes led to much embarrassment and laughter. I learned to laugh again but also learned to rely upon my intuition, my inner voice. Some strange, unknown force led me to the Isle of Wight, UK, where I immediately found a cozy bed-sit overlooking the ocean. The heating bills were too high, so I sought warmth in the research room at the library. When the librarian asked me what I wanted to study, something made me cry out, "God!"

This was the beginning of an exciting journey, a quest to discover who and what I truly am…a quest that took fourteen arduous years of research. It was then I stumbled upon an amazing discovery: through my intensive work I learned I was actually and inadvertently healing my brain through stimulating dormant neurons. Steadily and slowly, I grew in mental and spiritual awareness.

My chosen subject, the science of religion and the supernatural, changed my life and steered me towards a new way of thinking, opening a portal in my mind and led me to recently completing a 66,740 word story about my findings which I hope to have conventionally published!

Peace, however, was still a long ways away. A grueling court case led to one of the longest court battles in Canadian history, a battle marred by collusion and fraud, making both legal and medical history. Somehow I rose above it all, especially with the support of new, trusted friends, the deep love of my daughters, and my spiritual beliefs. Rising like a phoenix from my own ashes, I gained the compassionate capacity to embrace others suffering the devastating effects and grievous losses of brain injury.

Through my participation in the worldwide movement for brain-injury awareness, I enact change one step at a time. Especially by educating those cruelly prejudiced against the brain-injured and insisting upon and advocating modifications in outdated rehabilitation systems.

That long-ago misshapen face in the mirror is now a faded memory. In its place is another image: a strong determined crusader. From the hospital room of so long ago where I fought for my life, I now fight for the lives of others. I didn't give up then and I won't give up now.

Miracles Happen

Miracles happen, sometimes. One summer there was a group of people who prayed like maniacs for a young girl to recover from a life-threatening virus. They acted on their faith and their prayers were actually answered and the girl lives on. This is my story. That same summer, the same group of people prayed like maniacs for a 46 year old man and father of five, to survive a fatal diagnosis, and the man lives on only in memory. That man is part of my story too, he was my dad. While the mischievous pendulum of life weaves tales of life and death all over the world, this story begins in a quiet, northern New Jersey suburb.

To look at me lying on the hospital bed in a coma, you would see an ordinary-looking teen with brown eyes and a thick, curly mop of shoulder length brown hair that was matted down to the hospital pillow. I am certain that the sight of me: an unresponsive girl laying still on the hospital bed, pale skin, eyes slightly open, white tube protruding from mouth would make just about anyone feel the weight of an impending tragedy. Especially if you happened to pass by my room day after day and saw that nothing ever changed, except the nurses checking on me or the sight of my mother sleeping by my side.

You might wonder: How did this happen? What if I told you that there was no car; no bicycle; no soccer ball; no gang fight; no mosquito - no exciting story at all?

Just a 16 year old girl looking forward to her last year of high school and to life beyond New Jersey. I was a bookworm with big dreams. My face was usually burrowed behind a paperback or glossy college brochure.

I would write furiously in a spiral bound journal about my dreams, thoughts, poems, and stories. I could, and often did, get lost in the ideas, thoughts, words and imaginings hovering on the page. One summer day, the day I fell into the coma, August 20, 1984, I got lost in a dream-world for twelve days.

I was in my bedroom, stretched out on the bed reading. I had just eaten a cup of vanilla ice cream and I finally felt hopeful. I had been recovering from a case of pneumonia and had been feeling lethargic and queasy for days, but today I was able to sit outside in the sun and finally ate something more exciting than dry toast and apple juice. I read for a while longer before closing my book and turning off the light.

I slept for a few hours before I felt the need to call out to mom. It was the night the germ attacked, the night I slipped away. I called for help when I realized that I couldn't walk the short distance from my bed to the bathroom. I felt so tired, my arms and legs heavy with invisible weights pressing against every inch of my body. I felt dizzy, nauseous, and had a terrible headache. I was scared of the constant sensations of needles and pins pricking all parts of my body. "Mom, please come…"

We returned from the two minute arduous trek from the bathroom to the bedroom and I collapsed into bed. Both legs and both knees just gave out. Complete weakness. We did not say much to each other. I was too sick to communicate and she was just alarmed. What was happening to her daughter? She lay by my side and we both fell asleep hoping I'd improve by morning.

I did not. I felt dizzier and weaker in my legs and arms than the night before. My surroundings were beginning to fade. I tried to get up and to get dressed, but nothing worked. I could not get my arms to move or my legs to bend. I couldn't speak.

My parents sat me on the top of the stairway and pushed me down one step at a time. Then, each holding one arm, they led me into our brown station wagon, propped me up against the door (I could barely hold myself upright) and pushed me down onto the car seat.

Mom and dad left my four confused siblings at home staring out the window, scared again. They had instructions for what to have for meals (cold cereal or peanut butter and jelly) and what to do in case of an emergency (call the neighbor), but no explanations. All they knew was that another family member was being swept away unexpectedly to go into the hospital.

You see, as often happens, a double tragedy had hit my family. The pendulum had already struck once. Dad was dying from stomach cancer. Four months earlier, he was sent to the hospital to have his stomach removed. When the doctors found that the cancer had spread to other organs in his body, they sent him home, body intact. We were happy; he looked the same to us, at first.

We thought and wanted to believe that he was OK. If he would just stop eating potato chips, his stomach pains would go away and all would return to normal. Right? What did we know of death? I was soon to find out.

I remembered the drive to the pediatrician's office and the doctor's stern words, the last words I was to hear for days, "get her to the hospital, now."

Looking into the mirror that was hanging on the door while on my way out of the room, my brown hair was straggly and going in all directions. My eyes were glazed. I barely recognized this girl in the mirror. The sight of her terrified me. What was happening to her… to me?

This thought and all my thoughts just drifted away. All my energies were used getting back into the car and then to the hospital. I was put onto a bed; the nurses put a striped hospital gown on me, stuck an I.V. into my vein and took out my gold stud earrings. I worried about those earrings and feared I would never see them again (I never did).

My bed was wheeled into the hall way where I waited. Eventually, I was brought to a room with a big metallic machine. I had no idea what it was; it looked like a rocket lying on its side. When I was wheeled into it, lights began to flash around my head and then I was gone. Think of getting anesthesia before an operation. You are awake when you see the anesthesiologist, then you are nowhere, and finally you wake up in your hospital room.

This is similar to what happened to me, I was awake when I went into the machine, fell into a deep sleep, and at some point I thought I woke up, but I really didn't. I had fallen into a non-traumatic coma, and would lie there for the next twelve days.

The official diagnosis of my medical condition was encephalitis/viral meningitis, medical conditions where membranes of the brain become inflamed. According to the National Institute of Neurological Disorders and Stroke, "Encephalitis is an acute infection of the brain characterized by fever, headache, and an altered state of consciousness, with or without seizures. Most cases of encephalitis are caused by viruses."

This proved to be true in my case, though my blood was tested for mosquitos, rabies, ticks, and Reyes Syndrome no cause was found, just an unexplained virus that travelled to my brain. To everyone's frustration, no medical interventions were identified, other than the I.V. and the nurses who kept a check on my vital signs.

I could not be wakened, I did not respond to any stimuli, I had no gag reflex, and my pupils did not respond to light. I was unable to move and communicate with the outside world, but was trying desperately to. I saw the square florescent light bulb above my head. I had some awareness of my surroundings, but slipped in and out of different levels of consciousness. I saw the nurses, doctors, my parents, the hospital room and what was in it.

Sometimes, I knew when I was being pushed to one side of the bed and then the other in order to change the sheets. I could sense the different ways the nurses touched my body. Some nurses had a gentle touch; others were just fast and efficient. (Nurses, be gentle with your patients. They know.)

I had vanished into a tangled jungle of nightmares and prayers. I was entombed in a world of confusion and mixed messages: surreal images, fear and frustration verses determination, hope and sweet, joyous hymns; the demons verses the angels. A square metallic machine pops up one day. It is a ticking time bomb of my life. The machine beeps and flashes green, yellow, and red.

When I am doing well, the light flashes green, but when I have minutes to live a light flashes yellow. Red means death, my death. My closed eye fixates on this machine that actually sits beside my bed. Fear of the beeping was justified. I am told Mom fiercely objected to the respirator, so I was hooked up to the monitor. I am told it tracked my breathing and that a yellow light would blink and the machine would beep if my breaths became shallow.

Whoever was nearest to me needed to tap my chest, in the hope of reminding my body to breathe. Fortunately, my body responded to the tapping and I never went on the respirator. To this day, Mom wonders why the doctors did not recommend the monitor before the respirator, which was a far more severe intervention. I wonder what would have happened if she hadn't objected. I also wonder why no one told me that the machine was helping me. It would have been one less fear. (Nurses, talk to your patients. Visitors and loved ones, talk to the one lying there in silence.)

I often see my mom, Lucille, lying beside me on the bed, often in a yellow hospital gown. In my dream-world, she is LuAnn or Angel Lou, always my unceasing advocate. She is patient, gentle, insightful and courageous. She is always by my side, even though the doctors tell her to go home, even though she has four other children at home waiting for her while she waits for me.

I can feel the weight of her sorrow, I am near death and her husband is as well. I come to know that my kindly, lively, energetic dad will soon be dead and mom will be all alone. How can I let her lose a daughter as well? I feel strong pangs of understanding and resolve. I cannot let Mom lose both a husband and daughter. Were these the feelings that enabled me to break through to the conscious world or was it something else?

At some point, I see a gold cross hanging on the wall and my closed eyes choose to focus on it, rather than the creepy bulletin board, the evil nurse, or the beeping monitor. Despite the cacophony of death and paranoia filling my head, I feel comforted. On the twelfth day of the coma, I am told by my mother who was lying next to me waiting that I tapped her leg. I don't remember this, but it is what happened. My mom yelled out to the nurses. "She moved! Valerie has moved."

I finally broke through the invisible glass wall. I was immobile, my muscles atrophied. I could not swallow or speak. I could not move my neck, legs, arms, or fingers, but was suddenly on a path to recovery rather than the respirator. I knew who I was; I recognized my parents and the nurses. I was thrilled to be part of the world and was motivated to recover, even though it would be one small movement at a time with no guarantee of recovery. Somehow, I knew that the hardest part was over. I would live and would not die. It was called a miracle.

Life has been good to me and blessings abound: high school and college graduations, almost 20 years of a happy marriage, and two beautiful children. I feel angels and bask in moments of clarity and peace.

Learning to Like the New Me

Last year I thought the worst thing that could happen to me was to not have my plan work out. I was studying to get into a Communications program and I had to pass four subjects to qualify for a grade high enough to get assistance with my university studies. I also (finally) got engaged. I say finally because we had been together for seven years and had a mortgage for five. Let's just say I was very ready. I am also an avid actress. I was a highly stressed person with the aim to get married, study, and have a kid all by this point in time.

I work at a hospital in South Brisbane, Australia. I was working on the 4th of March in 2014, when I started to get double vision. Luckily (or unluckily), I knew to go to emergency. I spent a good part of the day there awaiting the results of a CT scan that was suggesting I had a lesion on my brainstem. I was transferred to another local hospital and they were pretty sure I had a brainstem caver Noma. A what? Well after googling, I found it is a cluster of blood vessels that look like a raspberry. I was in the middle of it hemorrhaging (hence the double vision). If you know brainstem surgery, it is not an area many surgeons wish to operate. I therefore had to take the wait and see approach - very scary when you know your brain is bleeding. I ended up in emergency another time in April of 2014, as I had numb fingertips (this was another hemorrhage and further growth of the lesion).

In May I called my parents (they live four hours away), to tell them I wanted this thing in my brain gone. To me I sounded normal but to them they could not understand a word I said. They told me to sit down and they were on their way (apparently they threw clothes in the car and raced to my home). I also called my fiancé and he couldn't understand me either, so he left work to come get me. I knew I would have to go to the hospital, so I packed my bag for a couple of days' stay (it ended up being four months).

I went to emergency on May 11th, 2014. By this time most of my body was numb, I had double vision, I was lethargic, I could not walk very well, I had hydrocephalus (water on the brain) and my left side was having tremors. I was in surgery two days later to have an EVD, which is supposed to immediately relieve pressure. I also had an angiogram to identify the location of the lesion in my brain. After this surgery I was unable to open my eyes, roll over, or talk. It was really felt that brainstem surgery can leave you with worse deficits than you started with, however, I was now almost dead. I had a craniotomy on the 16th of May, 2014. Apparently many people came to see the surgery. As a trained actor I thought I would become a rock star from being on television! Who knew it would be from having a rare problem?

I named my lesion Timmy. I had surgery sitting up, and was in ICU for four days, before I woke up. Over the next four months I had about six or so surgeries. I had meningitis twice in the hospital, and my final surgery was in July to insert a shunt. I had to learn to walk, eat, and talk all over again. There is nothing more attractive than a 27 year old using a wheelie walker.

Neurosurgeons are amazing at what they do, but they have no idea how to cut hair. I ended up looking like Joe Dirt's daughter by July. Oh yeah, I had a massively attractive mullet, lucky for me everyone kept telling me it was not that bad. When I got my emotions back, I finally realized how bad it really looked. I am not one to toot my own horn, but I used to have beautiful hair, I couldn't even hide it.

My hospital stay was made longer by what I would describe as my craziness. I believe if you have never had drugs before, and you end up on a hospital ordered concoction of drugs, you end up a looney. One night I believed a man and his family were coming to pour water on me. In the middle of the night I pulled my PICC line out (the one that goes in your blood vessel near your heart), filled up a water jug and escaped through the hospital. I could not find any damn phones to call my fiancé. I went out the front of the hospital, realized I would get in trouble, and walked back in. I ran into two security guards (they must have thought I was incredibly crazy) and I told them about my troubles. I was so angry they took me back to the ward. I ended up with security bracelets and posters of my face on the walls. Super famous again!

I also gained about 13kgs (28 lbs.) from being on steroids in hospital. Apparently the minute I ended up on full food again, I demanded takeaway every day. There was a point the doctor thought I was pregnant. When I got to rehab I told my sister that everyone was crazy and that the nurses were trying to kill me. I am not sure why she did not believe me.... I ended up pulling another PICC line out in rehab, and locking the nurses out of my room. I had to beg for the third PICC line and I really did need it. I was discharged on the 29th of August, 2014, a few days after getting off the wheelie walker.

We had to cancel our wedding for December 2014, as no matter how hard I try, a wig looks like a wig, though I have had some help with my image. These incredible hairdressers near home cut and colored my hair, and made me look so much better. With the help of the gym and my fiancé, I have lost about ten kilos. Apparently, what I went through was not like having a cold and I could not just return to work; I had to make many appointments and be cleared by many people.

At the moment, I am volunteering at the hospital that saved my life, and finally after a year and half I am back at work for three days a week. I am completely broke and still planning my wedding for next December. I had another MRI and found they could not get all of Timmy, therefore I am hoping for no more hemorrhages. Every day I wake up wondering if today is the day my double vision is gone, but alas, I still have to go out wearing my eye patch, until it leaves.

I live every day proving to myself that I have come far. I owe many people for my life. I recently trained hard for a stair climbing event, Climb for Cancer, and made it all the way up the 810 stairs. I also gathered a bunch of people to dress as pirates for The Mater Little Miracles walk on the 31st May, 2015. I had chocolate coins donated to hand out to the kids. It was a great day.

My plan now is to get ready for our wedding, study as a Paramedic and get back into acting. I have to tell you I cried for over a year about getting back to the person I was. It has taken so long to realize I did not like that person - I like the person I am now. It may sound vain, but I am very compassionate and understanding. I am kind. I am strong. I am not confrontational. I like the new me and believe that this was the best thing to happen to me. I will one day save lives, and previously I was making no mark on the world - I am now!

A New Perspective

I suffered a concussion in March of 2012 which caused Severe Occipital Neuralgia. Left untreated until February of 2013, I underwent a major surgery to sever nerves in my spine, in hopes of ridding my pain, and now I deal with nerve regeneration.

It's been a journey of pain, agony, tears, life changes, and loss of hope. But then there are times of serendipity, and the world slows down, and you notice the smallest of things you never would have before and how amazingly beautiful they are. You find yourself taking a deep breath of the crisp air on these coming cool mornings and for the first time you recognize how good that feels.

Those precious kisses and hugs from your grandchildren are even deeper than you thought they could get. It's these things you hold on to on the days and nights you feel you can't take it anymore. You reflect back to this and know you have to keep going and you want to. You tell yourself it's okay you forgot and it's okay you couldn't remember, you just keep finding the things that you never noticed before because you've been forced to slow down and now you can take the time.

You always miss the life you had, then you come to a point where you think you have accepted it and learn to appreciate what you can do that holds so much more value. However, for some reason, at some point, it always sneaks back into your mind: "I want my life back!", "I want to do this or that again", "I'm sick of being sick." Now it passes sooner and again you pull it together and realize that you are so blessed.

It can be a lonely world living with a brain injury. You can become lost in yourself because so many don't understand or it's hard for them to believe because you look so fine on the days they see you. So how could you be sick?

I have to take charge when it comes to this. I have to slow down, say no, make adjustments, and the big one: ASK FOR HELP. I just have to know I'm not the same person. A lot of me was lost in this three year journey, but I have also gained deeper inner peace. My eyes are opened to see the beauty in the smallest things, and I forgive and love even more deeply. I'm also blessed with family and friends that do understand my struggle and I don't know what I would have done without them by my side.

This is just another blessing in the midst of struggle, pain, and agony. I hope those of you suffering daily just to get by can learn to experience some of this, so you can keep it close and use it on those dark days and nights when nothing seems to help.

No Was Never an Option

The year 2011 started full of promise for me. Out of the blue and with no warning, a week into the New Year, I was struck down by a near fatal hemorrhage in the pons area of my brainstem. Surviving such a deadly stroke came with a very high price tag. I was given a 1 – 5% chance of survival.

My family was informed that if I survived the first forty-eight hours, I would need to come to terms with the fact that I would never walk again. The thought of being wheelchair-bound for the balance on my now unnatural life scared the living daylight out of me. With the odds stacked against me, I was determined to prove them all wrong.

After having spent some time in ICU, I was transferred to a semiprivate ward, where with the aid of a speech therapist I was taught to speak coherently again. Still numb, disoriented and overwhelmed by what had just happened to me, I was transferred to a rehabilitation facility where I would have to spend the next two months.

On admittance to the rehabilitation center, I was examined by a doctor and placed onto an untold amount of medication. For someone who had never taken so much as a pain killer before, I was suddenly on more medication than I care to think about, not to mention all the serious side effects that all these medications were causing me.

Accepting the reality of my future as a stroke survivor was the hardest thing I have ever had to contend with. This meant accepting that my life would never again be the same as it used to be. Disabled and filled with uncertainty, I was determined to learn to walk again. Against all the odds, I embarked on an intensive rehabilitation program. There was no stopping me now and I would spend every possible moment in the rehab facilities gym; working on those flaccid muscles of mine.

Six weeks after entering rehab, I was able to walk short distances with the aid of a four-prong crutch. One step at a time and with pure determination and perseverance, I eventually progressed to a single-prong crutch. Once discharged, I continued my intensive program as an outpatient at a local neuro-physiotherapist.

Soon after returning home, my marriage of fourteen years crumbled and fell apart when my wife took our two children and moved out. At the lowest point in my life, my family and friends abandoned me. With nowhere and no one to turn to, I was left desolate, without a support system. I was suddenly forced to face the daily challenges that the stroke threw at me on my own.

My stroke ultimately revealed the true colors of those around me. Through all the trials and tribulations, I have grown into a wiser, stronger and better person. I came to learn who and what is important in my life. Where ever possible I try to motivate and inspire other stroke survivors and their families.

Each year I have entered a fun walk, which is held by a popular local radio station, on the roads of Johannesburg and meanders through the scenic suburbs. At first I would walk as far as I could and use my wheelchair when I got tired. Last year I completed the full five kilometer walk without the use of a wheelchair or crutch. This was a huge achievement for me, especially after being told that I would never walk again.

Not once did I ever doubt myself that I would never be able to walk again. With the right attitude, I kept pushing on. A very large contributor to my success were the hours I spent in a Hyperbaric Oxygen Chamber (HBOT). I purchased and imported a portable chamber that I could use at home. Daily use with the recommended breaks saw enormous changes. Slowly sections of my brain and body appeared to wake up. After a while I was able to read more than a page of a book without getting exhausted. Combined with my intensive physiotherapy, the high tone started to ease off a little, allowing me to regain some gross movements back into my motionless limbs.

Five years later and after thousands of hours in the gym, I am able to get around, independent of a wheelchair or crutch. Although my balance is still severely affected, I do take things slow and those around me have learnt that when we walk, we get to do a high definition walking as we appreciate more of the scenery around us.

Life has been an uphill battle, but through it all I have learnt so much. This world is full of people with ugly characters, but thankfully they are the minority. They are outnumbered by those with good hearts and who are willing to be there for you. A positive attitude attracts positive people. Even with the limitations that I have, I have come to realize that the new people in my life are there for me and not for what I can offer them.

Shattering the One Year Myth

As the years continue to pass, I have gained one thing that I was not capable of having early on after my injury - I have gained a perspective that comes with time.

Like so many others who share my fate, I get a bit reflective every year around TBI anniversary time. It's a bit of a "take stock" time for me as I look at where I am today – compared to where I was. I now allow myself to look to the future with hope, a realistic hope that I will continue to heal.

But there was a day that someone stole my hope and left me completely and utterly devastated.

I'm a big fan of taking personal inventory. A year after I was struck down by a teenaged driver while I was cycling, I decided it was time. I'd heard a lot about neuropsychological testing. It was time to see how many of my marbles remained. I wanted a clearer understanding of my deficits so that I could have a starting point, a place to begin the next chapter of my healing.

After hours of grueling testing that took place over the course of several days, I sat down with my wife, Sarah, and the neuropsychologist. As we reviewed the results of my test, it was clear that my assessment was not quite what we expected.

"David, you are in the bottom five percentile in the areas of complex problem solving and verbal recall," he said as dryly as if giving driving directions to a stranger. This fact alone was shocking enough. But there were more sucker punches to my soul awaiting.

"You are permanently disabled, and any gains you have from here on out will be small at best," he shared, as my wife and I sat there trying to comprehend the gravity of his diagnosis.

Still keeping a stiff upper lip, I asked about scheduling a neuropsychological test a year out, suggesting that we could use this first test as a benchmark to measure future gains.

"There is no need, your gains will be insignificant at best," came the authoritative answer. As our visit wound down, there was a final hope-stealing shot across my bow.

"Most brain injury survivors see an IQ drop after their injuries. It's clear that you were a very intelligent man before your accident. Even losing some of your IQ, you should be able to get by relatively okay now," he propounded, as we were getting ready to leave his office.

Many years have passed since that meeting. Swimming in a sea with other survivors over the years, I have heard this same misinformation shared over and over again – after a year, you are as good as you are going to get. Please check your HOPE at the door. No need for optimism. Go directly to TBI jail, do not pass Go, do not collect $200. Hunker down and just grin and bear it. You are lucky enough just to be alive.

Balderdash!

As time continues to pass, I now recognize this kind of advice for what it is: old-school science. The old-school TBI science was simple and easy. After a year, any gains would be small. Thankfully, a new school of science is now dominating the national brain injury narrative. New school science embraces neuroplasticity and challenges the archaic belief that recovery has an end game. New school science embraces the hidden power of the brain and human body. New school science says that as long as you have a heartbeat, you will continue to heal. And best of all, new school science is a science of hope - hope that the way things are today are not how they will be next year, or in five years.

One of the first to push old school science to the side was Dr. Jill Bolte-Taylor. In her book, *My Stroke of Insight*, she speaks of measurable gains through the eight-year mark. Last year at this time, I attended a conference in Maine. The keynote presenter, who is also a doctor and the parent of a survivor, took to the podium in front of her peers and continued this new narrative.

"As a medical community, we got it wrong when we told you that recovery was over in a year. We got it wrong," she shared. You could have heard a pin drop.

I hold no ill-will, anger or resentment to the well-intentioned doctor who temporarily stole my hope. He was only preaching what his old-school science had taught him. As the tide continues to turn, more and more members of the medical and professional community are letting go of the one-year myth. The Dark Ages of brain injury recovery are slowly fading into the past. I need only look at my own life to see some of the long-term gains.

At two years out, my vertigo almost ceased. At three years out, I was again able to work beyond 2:00 PM every day. At four years out, I was able to read books again – something I thought I had lost forever. The list goes on.

Today I have real hope – hope that I will continue my path toward recovery. Not "whistling in the dark" hope, this is true hope based on my life experience as well as emerging science. I don't kid myself for a moment because I know I'll never be who I was.

But today, where I am going is so much more important than where I was.

Learning to Become Useful Again

I need to be useful again. I have repeated this phrase to myself hundreds of times since I received my TBI. I was in a car accident on April 1, 2001, while on my way to the large corporation where I had worked since I was 16 years old. The company was a grocery retailer and I started there as a bagger. I was 48 at the time of my accident, and had worked my way up in the company to Store Manager.

Through the years I held many positions such as Deli Manager, Assistant Store Manager, and many more. It was a highly responsible position that I held, and I was even selected by my peers to be the manager from my market area to serve on the executive counsel, meeting with the company President every month and representing the dozen stores in my market area.

I was always a planner: someone who had a plan to follow with desired goals in mind. Even when you plan, or try to plan, things can happen that you were not planning for or even expecting, as was my experience when I got my first job at 16 years old. It was just a job to make some money so I could do what I wanted in my free time and buy albums, concert tickets, and perhaps a car eventually. It didn't start out as a stepping stone for a career. It was just a job. I was a bagger at a grocery store, and worked hard. After I carried the cart of groceries out to the customer's car,

I would actually run back to the store so I could bag for the next customer.

I learned what hard work could get for me when I was promoted to the grocery department to stock shelves. The other baggers asked me, "how did you get into the grocery department?", because it was a more desirable position that they all wanted. It was then that I made the connection that it must be the hard work that got me the job in the grocery department.

I continued working for that grocery store all through high school, and even through college - in fact, I selected my college because I could continue to work at MY grocery store - and I thought of it as MY GROCERY STORE. I continued working there in the grocery department until a meat cutter spoke to me and said, "You should think about becoming a meat cutter. The pay is very good and it's a good job!" Another meat cutter had left his paycheck stub on the dashboard of his pickup truck and I could see that he was making over eight dollars an hour. When I started working, I was making $2.65 an hour. By this time I had gotten a couple raises and was making $3.15 an hour. I seriously thought I was making big money, and was actually concerned that I had to figure out what I was going to do with all that money!

I felt good about myself and my career…So, for many years I felt useful. I miss that.

I first tried to find a support group that might help me with my issues, but there were none in my area that supported high functioning people, so I started my own! We called it HI FI, which stood for head injury functioning independently. Being a part of the group helped me feel useful but it seemed to suffer from a decline in members and interest after a few months. So I kept searching.

I had a long history of being useful, but then I suffered a TBI and have not felt useful since. I am limited in my physical abilities but look for options to feel valued and contribute something. I volunteered at an animal shelter and a bookstore, but neither was helping me, so I continued the search.

With plenty of time on my hands I researched things that interested me. I watched a show on the internet about the life of Stephen Hawking where he said that everyone has something to contribute. I was inspired by his story and the accomplishments that he has made, despite his illness. So I continue to think there is something I can do. I hope that perhaps sharing my story with others who may be going through their own difficulties may help them to gain hope for the future.

One thing I gained from the support group was from asking others how they deal with their personality change. I said that I liked the old me but could not find him. Another member said that the old me was killed in the car accident and is never coming back, but now I have the ability to create the new me!

With that, I decided to stop looking at the past and concentrate on the future and work on making me a better person. Nothing can be gained by looking at my past and the wrong decisions I may have made and wishing things were different. Work on the future!

It seems that in the past 30 years I focused too much on my career and not enough on my family. Though it was my decision, and though I can rationalize the focus on my career for my family's benefit, I now realize that it was also for me and my own desires to be useful.

So now after my TBI, my wife wants a divorce and I have little relationship with my children because of my own actions prior to my TBI. But that is the past and I have to work on the future… and I will. Today I have hope that my best days are yet to come.

Living One Day at a Time

I am still a relative "newbie" in year one of a newly diagnosed TBI. First, a little about me - I am in my mid-fifties, a husband to a wonderful wife, and a father to a wonderful 17 year old girl. I guess you could say pre-accident that I was generally a "man's man". I liked to compete in outrigger canoe, dragon boat, and have represented the U.S. at a world-class level (Australia, China, and throughout Europe to name a few). I used to paddle my outrigger miles offshore in the ocean, especially after hurricanes on the east coast because the surfing was better.

I liked to snowboard, bike ride (I did a couple of "century" rides), surf, target shoot, and train in MMA (mixed martial arts). I played the ukulele, guitar, and hand drums. I worked out six days a week and was generally healthier than guys half my age! I did a lot of the cooking, especially grilling in the summer. I did my own landscaping and received many accolades from the neighbors for my yard. I completed many home improvements including replacing all of the windows in my turn of the century home. I worked as a science writer in the past and most recently as a Clinical Specialist in a neuro-ICU for fifteen years and I studied nursing as well. This all came to a screeching halt last March.

I was up snowboarding in Vermont with an ex-special forces friend. I remember arriving and taking a couple of runs. That was it as I "reportedly" wiped out and hit a tree. They thought I was dead at the scene. I was medevac'd by chopper to a trauma center in New Hampshire. There, I was intubated (eventually trached), placed in a "halo" vest, and had a feeding tube and PICC line inserted. My wife was driven to the hospital by a good friend. I spent approximately two to three weeks there. My wife now tells me that all of the staff in the ICU were great. They related to me as a fellow "ICU'er" and felt it could be any one of them lying there.

I was driven by ambulance with my wife at my side to a rehabilitation hospital closer to where we lived. My wife informs me that I started to have trouble during the long ride back and I informed the ambulance personnel that I was dehydrated and that they should hang an IV. They did and I improved. I don't remember.

My first recollection was probably about the second week of rehab. Suffice it to say, the staff including the nurses, aides, respiratory therapists, PTs, OTs, and Speech therapists were all wonderful. I spent three to four months there, with short stints to the regular hospital (where I worked, mind you) for an infection, etc. Even though I could go up on the roof deck at rehab to get fresh air, I longed to be outside. I was diagnosed with DAI (diffuse axonal injury), possible cervical spine damage, and a possible brachial plexus injury to my right arm. I had severe right-side weakness, speech difficulties, and double vision - all of which I'm still struggling with today. I was mostly confined to a wheelchair but used a cane during PT. Special glasses were made for me to aid in the severe double vision.

The Halo and cervical collar eventually came off as the ligament damage had healed, and the PICC, trach, and feeding tube were eventually removed. I was getting ready to go home!

I've been home now since August of 2015. I did go to outpatient therapy five days per week for approximately five weeks, then I went three days per week for several more weeks. I will start up again with PT, OT, and Speech Therapy in the spring. In the meantime, I get out of breath doing the treadmill (walking), stationary bike, rowing machine, and weights just about every day. I am truly happy to learn that exercise does benefit our diagnosis and I feel best on those days when I get in a good workout. I also read, both aloud and to myself every day, to work on the speech.

My thoughts on being home: IT'S WONDERFUL! The first thing I did was say hello to my dog. He really missed me! I have made it a point to get outside every day, even if it's a -5 degree wind chill. My wife has been great and she allows me to "test my wings" as it were without hindering me, although if you ask her, she was probably a little leery with some of the things I did. I've climbed a few rungs on a ladder and blew leaves off of my porch roof. I've hung a bannister (with my wife's help) downstairs to the basement. I've gotten the yard ready for winter. I've grilled chicken and salmon outside and taken the trash and recyclables out to the curb, albeit slowly, to name a few. All of these things make me feel alive, like I'm contributing something again.

My point to you as caregivers - let your loved one try things as long as they're safe. They need to feel useful and that they can still make a contribution. Those things I'm most proud of are learning to use chopsticks with my left hand, and changing a thermostat and light switch with my daughter and wife's help.

I was ecstatic when I didn't need the wheelchair, the commode, or hospital bed any longer. I was very happy when I could take a shower "standing up" instead of in a shower chair. I'm very happy to say that I haven't fallen even though I'm still quite wobbly. I do have bad days and times. Particularly before bed and when I wake up. You see, I still see myself as being able to do all of the old things in my dreams. It is a rude awakening to wake up to reality.

There are some things I hope will improve: I hope my voice improves so I don't sound like I'm drunk all the time. People tell me it's improving. We'll see. Even though I've had one eye surgery, I hope the double vision will continue to improve with glasses or perhaps another procedure. My follow up is in a few weeks. I hope my feeling or sensation will get back to normal, especially sensitivity to the cold (I always feel like I'm burning or heavy on the right side). I'd like to be able to drive again, for I do miss it. I hope when it gets nice that I can walk around the block without looking like I'm struggling (with or without the cane), and I eventually hope I can run and bike again! Some of the videos out there give me heaps of encouragement in this regard.

Everyone going through this wants to know, "does it get better?" I know that I wanted to know. If you ask people who have seen me at my worst, the answer is a resounding "YES!" If you ask me, I don't know? …as I sit here plinking away with one hand/finger. I know I won't be able to do all of the things I used to be able to do. But that's okay. I just hope I can do some of the things - one day at a time!

Journaling a New Story after Brain Injury

When a brain injury happens, the familiar story of a life can be altered in ways not possible with any other kind of injury or illness. So much you knew about yourself—the wealth of information you depended upon to lead your life—can blur or disappear, leaving you stranded and struggling in an unknown place. Along with cognitive and emotional challenges, you may face challenges with your physical abilities. You can feel as though you've been kidnapped to an alien planet where nothing is familiar and you are lost in dangerous territory.

Family caregivers can feel equally bewildered, as well as terrified. I certainly did when my husband sustained a serious traumatic brain injury more than a decade ago. But my journal offered a safe sanctuary where I could pour out my deepest thoughts and feelings without judgment or criticism. Writing somehow made them more manageable. Despite being diagnosed with secondary traumatic stress, journaling allowed me to hold on and cope with the overpowering uncertainty, fear, and anxiety.

As I've found during eight years of guiding journaling groups for people with brain injury and family caregivers, telling your story through journaling can enhance the healing process. "Healing" here does not mean restoring your injured brain to its former functioning or your life to the way it used to be. Instead, it means finding healthy ways to become aware of, accept, and acknowledge what has happened so that you can move forward into your new post-injury story. Journaling, for even five or ten minutes at a time on a regular basis, can help release you from yearning for the past and open positive doors to your envisioned future.

How to Journal

There are no rules in journaling, except perhaps to date all your entries. So don't worry about correct spelling, grammar, or punctuation. You need not be a "good" writer. Simply write in whatever way is comfortable for you. You can write on paper or use a keyboard. If a brain injury prohibits you from doing either, you can speak your entries into a recording device, use speech-recognition software, or find a trusted confidante who will scribe your words without judgment or changes.

Keeping your journal private allows you to write honestly. But if you occasionally write an entry that you never want anyone to read, you can tear it out and destroy it. The benefit of journaling comes in the writing, not in preserving what you write.

To begin, you can simply pick up your pen or put your hands on the keyboard. But it's helpful to create a structure for yourself by starting with a prompt (for example: Today I feel… or, the most important thing I can do now…). You can experiment with various techniques such as Dialogue or Unsent Letter, or even setting a time limit.

If you're writing about a traumatic experience, don't simply begin writing with no structure in place. Even something as simple as a five-minute limit can help you avoid writing yourself off an emotional cliff with no way back to safety. Stop writing if you feel yourself getting unusually upset. And over time, try to keep a balance between positive and negative so that you don't end up endlessly ruminating on the darker aspects of your life.

After a brain injury, you might not be able to write much or for very long. Do whatever you can, and please don't judge yourself harshly. As your condition improves, you will be able to write more. If you're a caregiver, you might have difficulty finding time for self-care, but know that you can journal in only five or ten minutes at a time. A small journal will fit in a purse or pocket, and you can write wherever you are.

As you continue journaling, you will have written memories of your healing and of how far you have come since brain injury altered your life. And there, in those words on the page, you—whether survivor or caregiver—have created the foundation on which to build the new story that will carry you into the future.

Healing your Heart after a Brain Injury

Winter can be a tough season for anyone but it can be exceptionally difficult for a brain injury survivor. On top of struggling with the winter weather, limiting outdoor activities due to the cold temperatures or slippery surfaces and the typical "winter blues", brain injury survivors are often struggling with a fundamental Life Crisis: who am I and what is my value if I can't do what I used to do, if my friends aren't my friends anymore and I'm a problem for my family?

Something essential that I learned and wish I'd known during my journey is that there is usually a grieving process associated with healing from a brain injury. I learned that there are common stages associated with the grieving process: denial, anger, bargaining, depression and acceptance. I also learned that processing grief is not a straightforward path, that one typically moves back and forth in the different stages and that is "normal." I learned that in order to heal and be able to move forward, it is necessary to recognize your feelings, acknowledge the losses, allow yourself to feel the feelings and mourn the losses.

The devastating losses brain injury survivors experience are far-reaching. On top of struggling with physical injuries and cognitive deficits, there are usually secondary losses as well: income, jobs, social networks, friends, even family and homes. Survivors often lose much of their life that took years, sometimes many decades, to build.

Needless to say, the changes and losses I experienced had a profound effect on me, on my Being. I found myself struggling with a fundamental Life Crisis: who am I and what is my value if I can't do what I used to do, if my friends aren't my friends anymore and I'm a problem for my family? I had lost my self-confidence and my "sense of self." I was becoming more and more depressed.

Something else to consider is that your family and friends may be grieving too. When you think about it, they have lost the person you used to be and the role you used to play in their lives as well.

Getting in touch with my spiritual guides was instrumental in helping me move through the grieving process and heal my heart. I needed to hear, to be re-taught, that I had value in my Being, not just in my doing. Being part of a support group for brain injury survivors let me know I was not alone in my struggle. Many find it necessary to seek professional help to cope with and navigate this complex process.

One of the keys for me was to forgive myself; forgive myself for not being able to do what I used to be able to do; forgive myself for being human. I also needed to forgive others for their shortcomings; for being human. Ignoring your feelings will hold you back.

Your grief and whatever way it manifests in your life will create stress and inhibit your rehabilitation process overall. Our brains work best when we feel well, physically and emotionally.

"We are human "beings", not human "doings." ~Bernie Siegel

Strategies that can be helpful:

♥ Keep a Grateful Journal, writing down three things every day that were successful, an improvement, or made you smile.

♥ Arrange regular get-togethers with friends, even if just to chat on the phone or to meet for a cup of coffee or tea.

♥ Spend some time on a hobby.

♥ Practice random acts of kindness.

♥ Volunteer.

♥ Get some physical exercise, every day.

♥ Go outdoors; soak up some fresh air, sunshine and vitamin D.

♥ Sign up for a class, anything that interests you.

♥ Think about what is most important to you and how you can bring more of it into your life.

♥ Keep your perspective, refer to your calendar and journals to look back and note improvements.

Celebrate what you can do now that you couldn't do six months or a year ago.

♥ Remember that you are still the same unique and valuable person inside, with the same loves that you had before your injury. No one and no injury can take that away from you.

Depression, like winter, is usually temporary, but if you feel like you are losing hope, please seek professional help.

Finding Gems in the Mud

It is so very hard to lose one's independence at any age. We hear stories of others, but no one ever thinks it will happen to them.

Not being able to walk far, drive, or take a bus, I am pretty stuck. I honestly have no idea how to do this. I take it one breath at a time. Free falling through space on my own, I have been searching for a way to manage this long-term. The system won't let me in Adult Day Care, I am too young. The swamis won't let me in an Ashram, I am too disabled. Searching for solutions, I actually did ask both.

My next idea is to search for a safe little town with good weather, one that has all I need within walking distance. I have just flown to a small town in Central California to see if I can function on my own here. The solo adventure itself is daunting. I pack barrels of courage in my suitcase.

As expected, three plane rides have shaken me up so badly that I can barely move or see. My vision has shrunk into a nauseating peep hole, and I can't tolerate moving my eyes at all. The slightest movement of my eyes disorients me and makes me even more seasick than usual. Information is not traveling from my eyes to my brain. It takes three hours to find my way around my tiny studio apartment. Expanding my world to the patio takes another few hours.

I have no idea how I will get groceries. Even at home, getting food is always the hardest thing for me. The over-stimulation of supermarkets causes my brain to shut down. Somehow, food always finds me when I really need it; like the Indian saint, Amma, who lived blissfully in the woods, animals and eagles dropping food in her lap when she was hungry.

Today's "eagle" takes the form of a friend of a friend who calls to welcome me to town. "The farmer's market is today, would you like to go?" She is an occupational therapist, she gets me. I hold on to her arm for dear life in the visual chaos of the crowd, and unexpectedly, I have produce!

It is magical the way my needs get met. I never have any idea how they will, but I am no longer living a rational life. I am grateful for the gem of kindness.

The farmer's market put me over my stimulation threshold, and I can't wake up. I get up once to take a shower which exhausts me so much that I fall asleep again; once to get dressed, which exhausts me so much that I fall asleep again; once to make coffee, which exhausts me so much that I fall asleep again… so much for caffeine. Finally at 2:30PM, I am awake.

Today, I will venture beyond my studio with the goal to find lunch. There is a café four blocks from here. Expanding my world beyond my apartment will be a big feat, beyond what anyone without a TBI can imagine.

Concentrating to get through the mental fog, I talk myself through it out loud. "Pull up walking directions on your phone. Study hard to make sure you have a sense of where you are going. Put on the green tinted glasses that relax your brain.

Check directions again. Put on the goofy Vibram toe shoes so you can feel the floor. I forgot the directions. Check directions again. Put on the hip belt full of rocks."

The hip belt reminds me of the confusion and alarm on the airport TSA agents' face two days before.

"What is this?"

"It is just rocks."

"Why are you bringing a fanny pack full of rocks on the plane?" she accused.

"They remind me where my body is. I am lost in space and my brain can't tell."

She had no idea what to do with that. I only brought one trekking pole on this trip. I need two. I look around the apartment. I find a broom stick. I am going out with a trekking pole and a broomstick. My life is ridiculous. I am thankful it doesn't still have the broom on it. That would be an odd picture. But I would do it with dignity!

I write up a little note, the way I learned in rehab. "Hi, I have a brain injury and I am lost. Can you please help me get to XYZ address?

If you touch my arm firmly, it will help me to get oriented to where my body is. Thank you!" I make sure my little notebook is open to the right page so I can pull it out (hopefully) when I can't move, read, or think.

Next, I get dressed up nice. This too, is a compensatory strategy. If I am relying upon strangers to help me, I don't want to look like a crazy person. I figure it is better to have them confused by me, than scared. "Always look your best, when you go out with a rock belt, toe shoes, green glasses, a trekking pole, and a broomstick!" That is my new motto.

Finally, I walk out the door for the giant four block excursion. I am so curious to see this town, but I have to be really careful not to look around and waste my little visual processing power. I pick a spot straight ahead and focus intently on it. Every half block, I rest, and hug a tree. Trees keep me grounded, they help me make my way through town. I have hugged so many trees in the last four years, they have become some of my best friends.

At the café, I find it is crowded and noisy, and I am about to topple over. I can't stay in this environment! A sweet blonde waitress cuts through the crowd toward me. "Hey sweetie, do you need some help with the menu?" She puts a firm hand on my arm. I smile, it's just what I needed - not only a nice person, but one who knew to touch my arm and remind me where my body is... as if she read my note. I thank her for her kindness and tuck it into my basket of things I'm grateful for today.

I collect gems like this as I go along. At the end of the day, I look back and admire my basket of sparkling gorgeous jewels that add beauty to my life. It is the kindness of people that fills my basket on a regular basis. It is what keeps me going.

Leaving the café, hungry, lost and completely disoriented, I get catcalled by a truck full of men. My life could not get any more ridiculous. Maybe my "look good when you carry a broomstick" motto has worked too well. Or maybe sleeping endlessly is the best beauty product ever. Apparently, my outer appearance does not at all reflect my fragmented inner state. This is both a blessing and a curse. I decide to appreciate the compliment, and tuck another colorful gem in my basket.

I find a bakery and buy some bread. Three blocks later, someone tells me that my purse is open and upside down. I had no idea. By now, my vision is incredibly restricted, and I have lost all sense of having a body.

I wonder how much money I have lost.

Grateful for this person, and for having bread, I put two more gems in my basket. My favorite sparkling multi-colored gem today, is the sudden realization that I have come so far with accepting a life without control that I can now laugh at the mistakes that previously had me crying for three years straight.

I have learned to trust, to stay in the moment, and to look for the good. I live by the mantra, "where attention goes, energy flows." When it rains, look for rainbows. I place my attention on the gems in my basket at the end of the day.

Happiness depends upon gratitude for even the smallest beauties of life. So what if I was walking down the street dropping all my money, I got bread today!

I had intended to visit the Unitarian church service to meet some people here. I can't wake up again. Frustrated and embarrassed, I arrive just in time for free coffee and food. I decide to forgive myself (it's a constant practice.) I go in anyway and hope the man I was talking to over pasta salad didn't notice that I picked up my fork by the wrong end - twice. My hand was gooey with dressing.

I have become one of those people: the people who wander into a church for free coffee and food. Yep, that is me today. This is my new life. At least I've eaten.

And I love myself anyway.

TBI living has taught me the biggest life lesson of all - to forgive myself unconditionally. I get so frustrated with myself, but I know that does not help me heal or thrive. I express it, let it go, and choose love and forgiveness constantly. I try to send my brain more love with every screw up. Sometimes it works.

Having a scrambled brain that can't get anything right, you have to laugh at your imperfections and find amusement in the absurdity of life. You have no choice. It's either that or jump off a bridge. I choose to laugh.

Like most of us, I have been driven my whole life by an intense need for perfection and belonging. Now, I have become so imperfect that I realize it is futile to keep striving for perfection. I wish I had known that it was futile all along.

I wish I had known it was ok to relax and just be me, warts and all. Not only am I imperfect, but I now write about it publicly, because I hope it gives life perspective and sets others free too. Limitation has never been so liberating. I am at peace.

Embrace the Day

Awareness is something we all take for granted, but on this particular day it was very important to me. I became aware that I was lying in bed. Scanning the room, I noticed I was in a single bed and behind a glass partition. There was a lot of activity beyond the partition but it did not yet register.

I turned to the other side of the room and saw my brother, Chris. Chris lives in Massachusetts, clear across the country from me. Now I was very confused. It did not make any sense. "What are YOU doing here? And WHERE ARE WE?"

Then I realized that I had a tube in my nose and wires in my arm and elsewhere. What the heck was going on?

Finally seeing my wonderful husband, Peter, I knew I was safe, but that still did not explain things. I was told (not for the first time apparently) there had been a horse-back riding accident, I was in ICU and had been there for THREE WEEKS.

After more days of recovering my awareness, this is what I learned:

On a beautiful autumn day, the scent of dry brush and a subtle sage wafted on the breeze. Bodhi, my horse, and I were trotting up the trail. And then it happened. As my friend Lori has told me, one minute I had Bodhi in an emergency stop, the next I was in the air on my way to a very hard landing – on my head. Not good. Paramedics were called and after they determined I had sustained a possible brain injury I was air lifted to USC Medical Center Intensive Care Unit.

After two months of ICU, hospital and rehab, it was another few weeks before I could go to the barn and see my horses. It was because of my relationship with them that I forced myself up to the barn every morning to care for them and, most importantly, to learn about how my new brain wiring would work, explore my deeper understanding of their communications, and to receive their healing energy. Not only were they helping me heal physically, they were helping me heal emotionally and energetically.

Instead of looking at my accident as "poor me, why did this happen?" I chose to look at it as a necessary experience and an opportunity to re-wire the neuro pathways in my brain so I can accept that I do vibrate at a higher frequency than others. My head injury was a necessary step in my life's journey of helping horses heal humans. Now that I am aware that I process things differently than I used to, when I'm working with my horses and they react to something I stop and wonder, "Hmmm, that's different. What is this about?" I check myself to determine if they are telling me something about me that I might not be aware of, or if something else is going on that I need to focus on.

Horses live life in the present moment, an important lesson that I have come to embrace. This is also tremendously helpful when we are working with clients. The gift of my brain injury is the new ability to be curious and see the joy in every day occurrences. Because I am able to work with horses daily I find that I smile a whole lot more, I have confidence in myself and I believe that my Equine coaching business is where my passion and joy lie. I get to assist horses in their healing of humans. Everyone benefits.

It has been a continuous journey. I had to re-establish my trust and relationship with both of my horses in different ways. It took almost a full year before Bodhi and I learned to trust each other again. We both know, acknowledge, and honor the realization that he has played an integral part in my life's journey. If not for coming off him and landing on my head, I would not have had the opportunity to re-wire the neuro pathways in my brain, spend three weeks in and out of consciousness as I explored my spirituality, and opened up the realization that the horses and I can help other trauma survivors navigate their way back onto their life's journey. It was because of my accident that I was introduced to the people I want to help the most - trauma survivors, and not just those suffering from TBI; all trauma survivors.

My mantra whenever I hit a speed bump in my path is: Pause, close your eyes, take a deep breath, smile and …Begin Again!

You never know when Spirit is going to offer up an opportunity. You just need to be open and receptive to issues and situations that at first glance seem random. For me it was the opportunity to be blessed with the friendship of horses. I believe that certain special things, people or animals come into your life when you need them the most. I had to gather the appropriate knowledge and life lessons before I would be ready and open to the healing gifts of horses.

A very important lesson that I have learned from this journey is that everything I do with and for my companions, be they two or four-legged, is a partnership based on love, trust and support. I trust my horses will be there for me, and they trust that I will lead them and keep them safe. I trust that all my clients have the ability to heal and grow, and they trust that I will support them and help them navigate through their process – no matter how long it may take or how difficult it may be. We are on the journey together as trusting, sharing, and caring partners.

My work gives me the opportunity to help horses heal humans. My husband, along with horses, mini burro, and dogs have our own facility ("Begin Again Ranch" Sedalia, Colorado) where we partner with my herd of wisdom horses. Together we coach people through life issues, trauma survival, self-esteem, relationships, empowerment, and grief and loss obstacles on their road to recovery. My business tag line "From Surviving to Thriving" sums it up completely. For me, TBI stands for To Be Inspiring.

My Journey to Regain Wellness

As I continue on my journey of health and recovery since sustaining my TBI, I have been inspired to travel down the path of diet and supplements. I really do not want to be on prescribed medications for an extended period of time. But right now, I am. I have tried almost ten different medications in the span of one year. Currently I am taking two medications daily to combat headaches and fatigue and executive function issues. I would say they are helping me to cope and survive the day, but I want to get back to thriving!

Interestingly I began my supplement journey about six months prior to sustaining my TBI. I began regularly taking a multi-vitamin as well as D3 and krill oil. Honestly, I'm not sure whether they made a difference. I continued taking these supplements after my TBI and when I was able to begin researching information on the brain and supplements, I added magnesium and turmeric. During a meeting with my neurologist I asked if these were harming or aiding in my progress. He said they were not harming me in the least, but there was no scientific evidence to show how they may be helping me. However, he suggested I begin taking 400 mg daily of B2 vitamins as there was current research at that dosage to support brain health. Vitamin B2 has been shown to reduce fatigue and depression as well as to improve memory. This certainly sounded great to me!

I honestly do not know if there is a difference in how I am feeling and thinking. Obviously, I have been improving since my accident and I am not sure if taking the vitamins and supplements have helped or if my recovery would have been the same. However, I am unwilling at this point to stop taking them to see how I would feel. I will tell you that after two months of taking these additional supplements, I had my annual physical and my primary care physician ordered various blood tests. One of the tests was for inflammation because of my chronic fatigue with TBI. The results were the best I had in years, so my doctor recommended I keep doing what I was doing.

The blood test for inflammation led me to begin doing some research in diet. I needed to get more fruits and vegetables in my diet in an easy way. I fortunately was able to go back to work, but with three children I had to find a way to eat more healthfully amid work, after-school activities, and supporting my children during homework. My employer happened to send out a flyer for South Shore Organics, which sends weekly organic produce to a designated drop off point.

The produce changes from week to week and recipe ideas are included. This worked for me! I didn't have to think about what to purchase, recipes to look up, or even go to the supermarket or Farmer's Market. I began roasting vegetables three to five times a week. My children have even found some new favorites and have asked for different dishes including those with squash, leeks, and kale!

I leave my home by 6:45 AM. Breakfast is not my thing - well, wasn't my thing. I looked into green smoothies on the internet and I began making Simple Green Smoothies. I signed up for a free 30 day challenge and I bought the book. I have now had a green smoothie almost every day this year. I love them and they start my day off better. There is some work to it, but as with all things related to TBI, once you have a routine you have conquered half of the problem. My routine is basically to cut up, measure, and place fruit in individual freezer bags each Sunday. I also measure out the kale or spinach and place that in individual baggies in the refrigerator. Before I had the routine down, I would leave the blender, recipe, and unrefrigerated ingredients on the counter so they were ready to go in the morning. As we know, setting yourself up for success post-TBI includes prepping the night before.

I feel I am only beginning my journey to regain wellness. I am planning to integrate an anti-inflammatory diet into my daily life. I currently am not drinking alcohol or soda, and my morning beverages are green tea as well as apple cider vinegar with pineapple juice. I use coconut oil and coconut aminos in cooking. But, I want to make clear that the changes I have made do not make me feel like I did prior to my motor vehicle accident. However, the plan is continued recovery so that eventually the healthy lifestyle changes I have implemented as a result of my TBI will become a positive out of a negative!

As with any dietary changes and addition of supplements, be sure to ask a physician before you take them. Many medications and supplements can cause adverse effects if combined with prescription medicines. This is my own experience and I am not a physician.

Left for This

A lot of people ask what it's like to have a traumatic brain injury. I smile and simply reply, "I don't remember." This is my attempt of adding humor to the truth. Most don't get it. I suppose it's one of those things you only get if you've been there.

I have a hard time explaining what it's like to have my brain no longer function as it did, to learn new ways and strategies to be able to function throughout a day. Daily I live with the struggle and frustrations from feeling as though I lost who I was.

My injury occurred when my car's air conditioner was blowing my hair as it blasted away the hot July heat. It was one of those humid days that fog your sunglasses and causes you to sweat the moment you step outside. Scouring the storage unit for a house plan was the last thing I wanted to do. Especially since my workload back at the office was more stifling than the heat.

I didn't mind traffic was backed up on the highway. There is something restoring about being all alone in the car, listening to music, with no one to interrupt my thoughts. It's like a salve for life, which makes me wonder what's wrong when I need it so bad.

I should be happy, getting where I wanted to be, only now the feeling in my soul tells me something's missing. I miss God. I miss feeling Him strong and powerful, and moving. I don't like how small He is in my life, and how He can conveniently be compartmentalized according to my plans. That's not God, it's just one more thing to do.

Stuck out there on the highway, I began to pray for God to do something. To move. To make a way because there didn't seem to be one. I was caught in a life I intentionally set up, one God was a big piece of, and I was ready for God to take over.

As "Amen" left my lips, so came the impact from behind. A kid texting and speeding in a SUV never looked up.

The high speed sent my body whipping back and forth.

I should have prayed specifically. Obviously God slotted me into the wrong category. Getting hit by a car wasn't what I had in mind... couldn't it have been more along the lines of teaching Children's Sunday School?

The timing of the accident was too perfect. God takes months and even years to answer my prayers, but He must have been in heaven lining up cars, waiting for my final word. Obviously this is a test. No, I would not throw the car in reverse, and back over the guy who hit me while texting. No, I would not be irritated; he lacked manners and compassion, and didn't get out of his car to check on me. I would show mercy and grace, knowing he probably regretted a stupid mistake. God knew what would happen, so I'd choose to be thankful for His timing and the given opportunity to extend grace.

Having never been in an accident before, I couldn't believe I could be whipped around like a rag doll and not be hurt worse than I was. The officer on scene and the doctor in the Emergency Room warned me how bad it would be especially with such a hard impact.

It was tiring the way people made a big deal out of nothing. I had lived through and endured a lot of pain. This really wasn't so bad. Naively I assumed a sprained neck would be like an ankle – I'd feel it right away.

The next morning I woke up with the room spinning and when I tried to sit up I couldn't lift my head off the pillow. Had I not been so convinced sitting up would help the dizziness, I would have stayed down, but my stomach was turning and was hot like I was motion sick. It hurt to lift my arms high enough to use my hands to support my neck. I slowly sat up hearing the officer's words from the day before, "You will feel every one of those miles per hour tomorrow." My hands shook as I looked for the strong pain-killers the doctor prescribed.

Standing in the hot shower, the water mixing with my tears, I didn't dare let go of my neck. Like an infant, my head was too heavy to hold up. If it tipped and I used my neck muscles, it sent me through the roof. I retracted every thought I've ever had, about any level of pain tolerance.

I started sleeping over twenty hours a day. I would eat and fall asleep while chewing. I couldn't force my eyes to stay open when someone was talking to me. It was a lot like waking up from anesthesia. I was told the whiplash was the most severe it could be, just short of snapping my neck. None of it really phased me. All I wanted to do was take some more pain pills and muscle relaxers and go to sleep.

Everyone assumed my drowsiness was due to the prescriptions and bodily injury. A week and a half later I stood in the middle of an aisle at Target, and came undone. My body wash had been repackaged. I didn't know if it was the same, I didn't know why it was changed, I didn't know if I'd like it. What kind of jerk changes a girl's body wash? As I stepped back and looked at all the shining bottles lining the shelves, I started to panic.

The thing is, I knew it was crazy. I knew it didn't make sense to cry. But it didn't matter. I couldn't stop.

I went in to see my family doctor. She mentioned something about brain injuries during accidents and how I'd have to go to a rehabilitation hospital and would not be going back to work for some time. I heard her words, and they terrified me. As a single mom I couldn't be missing work. I cried, knowing as an inconvenience I'd be fired. To me, it didn't make sense why family and friends were freaking out about a brain injury. My job was on the line.

The day of the appointment with the traumatic brain specialist at the rehab hospital was one of the worst days of my life. I freaked out and didn't want to go.

There was something wrong with me and I knew it. I didn't need anyone else to tell me what crazy is. Besides, I would have to get dressed to go and I couldn't. I laid in bed in a heap of clothes crying. I didn't know if I should wear a tank top or short sleeves. Although it was August, I worried about the hospital being cold and if I needed to bring a jacket, or wear jeans. On top of that, there were so many colors to choose from. How do I pick the right things? How do I know what I pick is right?

I began wondering what the hospital does with crazy people. Do they lock them up, drug them, and take away their children?

I looked at the doctor debating if I could trust him enough to tell him what was going on. I couldn't keep my thoughts straight long enough to do so. My mind was so garbled. Humiliation burned my cheeks knowing the nurses probably told him I was in tears handing back the medical forms I couldn't fill out. Not seeing other options and knowing I needed help, I laid it all out.

The headaches which never go away. Feeling as though someone took a potato peeler to my brain, it hurt so badly.

Sleeping over twenty hours a day.

Nausea and dizziness. The bed spins and rocks when I'm laying down. Closing my eyes makes the bright lights come.

Ringing in my ears.

Static vision - like I'm looking through an old television.

Sensitivity to light, sound, movement.

Can't quit crying.

Can't follow conversations. Be talking and suddenly not know the next word I was going to say or what I had just said, or what the conversation was even about. I can't find the word I'm looking for or need to say, but can define it.

Can't make decisions or know what to do.

When I finish speaking, the doctor looks up from his notes and tells me I'm not crazy. I don't buy it. He tells me I have a traumatic brain injury. He looks at me and I can see a sense of sadness in his eyes, but I don't understand why. I'm going to get better. I'll be just fine.

At the first appointment I had with the Speech Therapist, she asked if anyone told me I sheared my brain.

Of course not. I did what?

She looks at me and says the doctor probably went over it with me. I'm at a loss for words because if he did, I didn't remember.

She explains to me how the brain sits in fluid and when it's whipped back and forth suddenly, say hit from high speeds from behind, the fluid can't protect the brain. The brain hits and rubs against the inside of the skull.

Another word for it is Diffused Axonal Syndrome. The pathways in my brain are strained or broken. Some will heal with time, some will reroute, but what I don't regain I'll be shown ways to handle and deal with it.

For the first time, it dawns on me I'm not going to be ok. This isn't the flu, it isn't a cold, or a broken bone. I'm not going to be the same.

No way will that be me. I'm not going to turn out like everyone else. I'll do whatever it takes and I'll get better. I'll figure it out and be just fine again. I'd join the ranks of those the doctors told would never walk again, and then they did.

I leave my car running. I can't find my kids when they're in the basement playing. I get lost in my neighborhood, on my block, on my street. I blow dry my hair but don't stop until my scalp is burned and my hair crunches. I freak out in a thunderstorm. I lose my train of thought and can't remember what I'm talking about or what people are trying to tell me. I talk to someone I haven't seen in weeks and they talk about what we did yesterday. I'm a mess.

I tell the doctors they need to do something. There is something terribly wrong with me. I'm supposed to be getting better, but I'm getting worse. As I tell them, I pray there is something they can do to make it stop. To halt its progress and get the damage to reverse.

The brain injury specialist smiles and tells me I am getting better. Obviously, he's not listening. In frustration, I start over, telling him what's wrong with me. I beg him to understand so he can figure out how to fix it.

His smile changes to a serious look as he tells me it only feels like I'm getting worse, but in reality I was so far gone before to know how bad off I really was.

I believe what he says. I lean against the back of my chair and take a deep breath. He continues to talk and I know I should be listening but I can't.

All I can think about are other times in life when I've been as truly terrified as I am now. There aren't very many.

The hardest thing about living with a TBI is that feeling what I do, doesn't feel like me. As though everything I do is wrong, merely because it's not the way I've always done things. The way I think and learn and retain information, isn't the same.

I always figured if I had to relearn how to think or do things, it would be in my old age from a stroke. Then, I'd have plenty of time to do that during the day. I didn't know it would happen from a brain injury in my 30's while I'm a single mom with young kids to care for, and a demanding job.

A lot of people try to be optimistic and hopeful. They tell me I'll figure it out; I'll get through this time and learn a new norm. It fails to encourage me, but it strikes a chord of anger and resentment. Because if it's that easy, I would have done it by now. And maybe since I haven't, I've failed at that too. However I end up might be okay for others, because they're not the ones having to live like this.

Acceptance hasn't come as a sudden decision. Acceptance started to come in small little ways at times where it didn't hurt me anymore to have to use obnoxious time-consuming strategies. When my resentment of them diminished and against all odds, I started embracing them, needing them, and not hating myself for it.

I had to learn to lower the bar and give myself a break. It was hard, I wanted to be the same person I've always been. The problem is, I'm not.

I started letting go of frustrations and getting upset, I couldn't do what I wanted to. Being angry and upset wasn't getting me further along. As I did, I started to gain excitement in my accomplishments. Because there are accomplishments. No matter how small and pathetic they may seem, they're huge. They're what gets you to the next. They lay the foundation. Once I understood and felt it, I started to be proud of my progress.

There is also a discipline to learn. Sometimes I'm busy and I'll think I won't have to use a strategy, such as writing something down to remember. But I'll forget it. I have to do what I know will be successful no matter how small it may seem. It's worth feeling good and confident, instead of frustrated and upset.

"The harsh truth is there are no benefits, no positives, for brain damage", I still remember the pressure in my chest hearing those words. I snapped back at the doctor, "I like things sugar coated."

The doctor went on to explain that even a heart attack can lead to someone feeling better, but brain damage is never good and doesn't provide benefits. Ever.

He might be right in the medical sense, but I will tell you he's flat out wrong in others. Life has never been harder, but I also love and appreciate so much more about it. I take better care of myself now than I ever have. I'm aware of how events and situations affect me.

Walking around feeling a little broken can make you more aware of the brokenness in others. Even those who are blind to it themselves.

I thought when the year mark hit and the vast amount of healing had taken place already, I'd be depressed. But I wasn't. I was truly happy. I wasn't where I wanted to be (back to pre-accident self) but I made it. I had learned to live again. I thought about all 365 days I had endured, and my sense of accomplishment soared.

Having a traumatic brain injury, has made me fearless in ways. As hard as it's been to survive and get back to life, I know I can face anything. The empowerment I've gained has been unreal.

What I have to remember is I'm still me. Maybe I'm not exactly the same, but I don't need to be. God doesn't need my strengths and abilities to use me. He can use us all, right where we're at, in ways we never could have imagined.

Meet Our Contributors

Nancy Bauser is a disability life coach and the owner of Trauma Recovery Expert LLC. Over forty-three years ago – in 1971, Nancy sustained a severe closed head/brain stem injury while attending undergraduate school. A longtime resident of Bloomfield Hills, MI, Nancy maintains an active profile in the community and supports organizations that benefit healthcare recipients. You can read more of Nancy's work here: www.survivoracceptance.com.

Donna Becke is grateful to be able to share her experiences as a traumatic brain injury survivor. Donna currently resides in Kentucky and loves spending time with her family.

Patrick Brigham is the resident cartoonist for TBI HOPE Magazine. Most every month, Patrick takes us on adventures with Hope, and her constant companion, Faith.

Steve Brydon is a traumatic brain injury survivor originally from the White Mountains region of New Hampshire. Steve is the founder of the HI FI Brain Injury Support Group. Steve prides himself in being "at the ready" to help any survivor in need.

John Byler survived a collision just outside of Boston in September of 2005. He placed his recovery in the hands of Spaulding Rehabilitation Hospital in Boston. John knew he needed to write a book about the best of the strategies he learned. *You Look Great! -Strategies for Living Inside a Brain Injury* has resonated with survivors, caregivers and clinicians.

Laura Chagnon is a freelance poet and brain injury survivor. Laura Chagnon continues to craft poetry each day with plans on publishing her second book of poetry. Laura's book is available at Barnes & Noble.

Amiee M. Duffy is the proud mother of three children. She has been teaching for over twenty years and is looking forward to using what she has learned about Executive Function and Working Memory in order to better serve all students in her classroom.

Grant Evans was born in a town called Barrow-in-Furness, which is located just south of the lake-district in North West England. Grant spent the majority of his life in Barrow-in-Furness, apart from 7 years as a child in Sydney, and the past 5 years of his life in Brisbane, Australia. He enjoys living in Brisbane because it has such a relaxed vibe and he has made some amazing friends there – friends for life!

David A. Grant is a traumatic brain injury survivor from Salem, NH. In addition to publishing TBI Hope and Inspiration Magazine, David is also a staff writer for Brainline.org as well as a contributing writer to *Chicken Soup for the Soul, Surviving Traumatic Brain Injuries*. David is the author of *Metamorphosis, Surviving Brain*

Injury. For more information about David, please visit www.metamorphosisbook.com.

Cheryl Green, MFA, MS integrates her degrees in Performance as Public Practice and Speech-Language Pathology to explore how story can be used to break down stigma and barriers through film, podcasting, and blogging.

Natalie Griffith was brought back to life and given a second chance at life on Christmas Day. She has been working on relearning how to be a mom and interact with her children. Says Natalie, "I love to make things pretty, BEAUTIFUL, so I have started a cleaning, organizing, straightening job; bathrooms and kitchens are my specialty. Never, never, never give up!"

Donna Hafner is a survivor in the truest sense of the word. Coming back from near death and living life as a brain injury survivor have validated why those closest to her know her by her nickname – Resilynt.

Kylie Hammon is a freelance writer and blogger. She lives finding light in tragedies, and encouraging others to believe there's a plan. God can bring good where there is none. Her smile and confidence inspire the least likely to believe. Kylie lives a very real life in Nebraska with her two kids.

Nancy Hueber, professional pianist, wife, mother, and frequent visitor to her couch and bed, survived a near baseball-sized brain tumor (meningioma) in the middle of her brain, and its removal by craniotomy six days later. In 2012, Nancy and her husband Tom established a brain injury support group in their town in northeast Missouri, now affiliated with the Brain Injury Association of Missouri.

Mike Jennings is a TBI survivor and has been a Support Group Facilitator for BIAC since 2005. Previous to his injury he served as a project engineer for Hamilton Sundstrand. Mr. Jennings currently serves on the Aging & Disability Commission for the Town of Simsbury and on the Board of Directors for New Horizons Village, an assisted living complex in Unionville, CT.

Nathalie Kelly was a Board-Certified Hypnotherapist before her TBI. Nathalie now publishes a blog and she speaks publicly about brain injury. She has educated others about brain injury on the radio, news, and the Oprah Winfrey Network. This month, she is launching her new YouTube Channel and Website, www.TheTBICoach.com as a gift to brain injury survivors.

Dr. Katherine Kimes is the President of ABI Education Services, LLC, and is a Certified Brain Injury Specialist. ABI Education Services is a business focused on providing consultation, training, in-school support, and transition services to children, adolescents, and young adults with acquired brain injury. Please visit her website at www.ABI-EdServices.com for more information.

Sara E. Lewis, M.A., M.B.A, M.S., has lived an eclectic life, skipping from jobs in museum management, to business management to education to healthcare. She is married, has four children, four grandchildren, and a dog. She is dedicated to spending the rest of her brain-injured life doing whatever she can to help persons with brain injury. Her memoir, *Not What I Expected: My Life with a Brain Injury (I Didn't Know I Had),* was published by Lash and Associates in May 2015. She blogs about all things at the intersection of brain injury and speech-language pathology on her website at thebraininjuredslp.com.

Brian Maram is a Traumatic Brain Injury and stroke survivor from Johannesburg, South Africa. Brian takes pleasure in motivating other stroke and TBI survivors. He is in the process of writing a book about his journey.

Joan Miller lives in Portland OR with John, her husband of 23 years. In addition to her busy speaking schedule, she volunteers at Oregon Impact and Good Samaritan Hospital. Joan is well known in the Portland Oregon vicinity for her passion for teaching people to find significance in their lives and to recognize the value they have to offer. Joan's website, blog and more can be found here www.JoanWins.com.

Terri Mongait is a Trauma & Transitions Recovery Specialist. She is also a traumatic brain injury survivor and has personal knowledge of the journey to recovery. Terri has over 20 years of experience in the corporate world at The Walt Disney Company and now uses her skills to help others. To learn more about

Terri's work with horses, visit www.BeginAgainRanch.com.

Norma Myers and her husband Carlan spend much of their time supporting their son Steven as he continues on his road to recovery. Norma is an advocate for those recovering from traumatic brain injury. Her written work has been featured on Brainline.org, a multi-media website that serves the brain injury community. Her family continues to heal.

Drew Palavage takes pride in being a good husband and father. He is also a fierce competitor and works hard every day. Right now he enjoys working out and maintaining his home.

Wendy Proctor is a traumatic brain injury survivor from Belleville, Ontario, Canada and is still learning and growing through her art.

Rosemary Rawlins is the author of *Learning by Accident, A Caregiver's True Story of Fear, Family, and Hope.* She is also Editor of BrainLine blogs and a national speaker on caregiving topics. You can learn more about her at: www.RosemaryRawlins.com

Melissa Robison holds a Bachelor's in Accounting and Master's Degree in Technology Management, she is a recipient of the Massachusetts Women in Public Higher Education Award, and a featured Student of the Week at Bridgewater State University. A traumatic Brain Injury and PTSD Survivor, Melissa continues to give compassionately though she has debilitating daily heath conditions. Melissa served as a member of a highly respected Spiritual Group in Massachusetts, where she volunteered Medium and Healing services.

Doug Rowe is a brain injury survivor from Red Deer, Alberta, Canada. When he's not writing about his experiences as TBI survivor, Doug enjoys time with his dogs K'Ehleyr and Dima.

Deborah Schlag is the author of the award-winning book, *Becoming the Healer, The Miracle of Brain Injury*. Deborah lives in North Carolina with her husband where she has founded Awakenings Center for Inner Healing & Empowerment – a non-profit healing center to bring healing to others and empowering them to move forward in their own healing process. Her story has also been featured in *The Resilient Soul*.

Jeff Sebell is a long-time TBI survivor. He is the author of *Learning to Live with Yourself after Brain Injury*. You can read more about Jeff and his journey on his blog at www.TBISurvivor.com.

Shannon Sharman was born in Perth Western Australia and now lives in Brisbane Australia. Shannon has been with her fiancé for eight years and planning on a 2016 wedding. She has a real passion for acting, and loves going to the movies. She has a love for charity work and is a volunteer at the hospital that saved her life. Next year she intends to study paramedics.

Barbara Stahura, Certified Journal Facilitator, has guided people in harnessing the power of therapeutic journaling for healing and well-being since 2007. She facilitates local journaling groups for people with brain injury and for family caregivers. Co-author of the acclaimed, *After Brain Injury: Telling Your Story*, the first journaling book for people with brain injury, she lives in Indiana with her husband, a survivor of brain injury. To learn more about Barbara, please visit www.BarbaraStahura.com.

Carole Starr is a motivational brain injury speaker as well as both Founder and Facilitator of Brain Injury Voices. She can be contacted through the Brain Injury Voices website at www.BrainInjuryVoices.org.

Michael Strand has lived with brain injury since 1989. Michael shares his experience though his written work including several books and his brain injury blog. Michael is also a *Chicken Soup for the Soul* contributing writer.

Jessica E. Taylor is the author of the books, *The Journey Back* and *From Tragedy to Triumph: Journey Back from the Edge.* She is an activist for Head Injury Awareness, and was honored to have been featured in the Betty Clooney Center Newsletter, March 2013. She was also featured on the Hidden Heroes documentary film on Canadian TV as well as several National TV and radio chat shows in both the North and South of Ireland.

Valerie Van Selous is happily married and a mother of two teenagers. She is earning a living working for a small non-profit, but her passion continues to be reading and writing. She is proud of her volunteer position as a Reader for the journal Creative Non Fiction.

Barbara J. Webster is author of *Lost and Found, A Survivors Guide for Reconstructing Life after a Brain Injury*, Lash & Assoc. Publishing and a contributor to Chicken Soup for the Traumatic Brain Injury Survivor's Soul.

Jennifer White is a traumatic brain injury survivor from St. Louis, Missouri. When she's not writing about her life as a survivor, she enjoys spending time with her family and of course, quilting.

Amy Zellmer is a writer, photographer, coach, and TBI survivor. Located in Saint Paul, MN she is a regular contributor for the Huffington Post. She enjoys traveling the country with her Yorkie named Pixxie. She loves chocolate, Miss Me jeans, Starbucks, and everything glittery and sparkly.

TBI HOPE

Offering Hope & Inspiration Daily

Follow TBI HOPE on Facebook

Join over 20,000 members in one of the largest TBI support communities worldwide.

www.facebook.com/TBIHopeandInspiration

Get your Free Subscription to TBI HOPE Magazine

TBI HOPE Magazine is a free, all-digital monthly publication supporting all affected by traumatic brain injury.

www.TBIHOPEMagazine.com

Made in the USA
Charleston, SC
04 August 2016